# Modernisation and Decentralisation of EC Competition Law

# European Business Law and Practice Series

VOLUME 16

*The titles published in this series are listed at the end of this volume.*

European Business Law and Practice Series

# Modernisation and Decentralisation of EC Competition Law

Edited by

## José Rivas

and

## Margot Horspool

Associate Editor
**Benoît Keane**

**Kluwer Law International**
THE HAGUE/LONDON/BOSTON

*Published by:*
Kluwer Law International
P.O. Box 85889, 2508 CN The Hague, The Netherlands
sales@kli.wkap.nl
http://www.kluwerlaw.com

*Sold and Distributed in North, Central and South America by:*
Kluwer Law International
657 Massachusetts Avenue, Cambridge, MA 02139, USA

*Sold and Distributed in all other countries by:*
Kluwer Law International
Distribution Centre, P.O. Box 322, 3300 AH Dordrecht, The Netherlands

**Library of Congress Cataloging-in-Publication Data**

Modernisation and decentralisation of EC competition law / edited by José Rivas and Margot Horspool.
    p. cm. – (European business law & practice series)
    ISBN 9041114424 (hard cover: alk. paper)
    1. Restraint of trade—European Union countries. 2. Antitrust law—European Union countries. 3. Competition, Unfair—European Union countries.  I. Rivas, José.
II. Horspool, Margot. III. Series.

    KJE6456 .M64 2000
    341.7'53—dc21                                       00-059309

*Printed on acid-free paper*

ISBN 90-411-1442-4

Printed and bound in Great Britain by Antony Rowe Limited.

# Contents

# Foreword

This book is the result of a Conference held in London in September 1999, jointly organised by Hammond Suddards Solicitors, who also gave generous sponsorship, and the Centre for the Law of the European Union of University College London. This conference followed on a similar event the previous year on the Europeanisation of UK Competition law and many of the papers refer back to this conference.[1]

Much has happened since the last conference and the papers reflect this. The conference on Modernisation and Decentralisation of EC Competition Law was amongst the first, if not the first, to address the issues surrounding the European Commission's White Paper published in April 1999 (see annexe). In this respect, the conference presented distinguished speakers with their first opportunity to air their views in public on this important development in the evolution of competition law in the European Union. The Editors have tried to cover as much ground as possible, giving the views of authoritative contributors and competition authorities from most of the major European countries and from the European Commission. The contributors naturally focus on the Commission's White Paper and view their national situation in this light. There is extensive treatment of the situation in the UK and the entry into force of the UK Competition Act.

The Commission's White Paper has led to a number of very interesting debates regarding the modernisation and decentralisation of EC competition law. The Editors are very grateful to the contributors for their interesting and provoking analysis of the subject and hope that, as the debate has only started, this book will provide a valuable contribution.

London, 14 March 2000                                          **Margot Horspool**
                                                               **José Rivas**

---

1 'The Europeanisation of UK Competition Law', September 1998. Book of the same title published 1999, Hart Publishing.

# Chapter One: Modernisation and Decentralisation of EC Competition Law

GIUSEPPE TESAURO[*]

## I

The Commission has always been the principal promoter of competition and free market in the European system, much as the Community's rules and regulations have provided the legal framework for assessing the conduct of undertakings. There are good reasons why this is so. In many, or rather, most European countries competition policy is not grounded in a long-standing tradition nor it is deeply rooted, and therefore it was only natural that the thrust and direction towards the opening up of the markets was provided for by the 1957 Treaty of Rome. Within the context of a broader liberal orientation, competition is represented in the Treaty as a statement of principle, and is to be found among the 'implications' of Community action. It is among the Community's primary objectives and at the same time it is identified as one of the instruments the purpose of which is to maintain and consolidate an integrated and unitary status of the market.

This latter aspect of Community action was most probably a priority in the original design. Moreover, whether competition was considered as an absolute value or as a common market instrument, the relevant rules were regarded as a means to guide undertakings towards fair competition practices and direct consumers towards the choice of higher quality products and services at appropriate price. On the other hand, in this context, which was finalised by the creation of a single market, while at the same time allowing Member States to assume full responsibility in shaping their economic and monetary policies, the safeguard of competition provided the opportunity and the basis for developing some fragments of a common industrial policy. Such was undoubtedly the effect generated by the existing framework of competition rules, which essentially consists of prohibitions, leaving ample scope for monitoring activity and for the judiciary's involvement; as well as by the Commission itself, which has been able to implement true competition policy through a far-reaching use of exemptions as provided for by Art. 85(3), now 81(3).

In this context, the enforcement of the rules set forth to safeguard competition were entrusted to the Commission. Its task was to convince the Member States to adopt a 'new' value or, in any case, to adopt a value which had always been considered of marginal relevance. The objective was to introduce a number of criteria, and the subsequent implementing rules, which would ensure a uniform application of

---

[*] President, Autorità garante della Concorrenza e del Mercato, formerly Advocate-General, Court of Justice of the European Communities.

*J. Rivas and M. Horspool (eds), Modernisation and Decentralisation of EC Competition Law*, 1–12.
© 2000 *Kluwer Law International*.

the Treaty's provisions throughout Member States; criteria which above all were designed to be consistent with the goal of unifying markets, and precluding undertakings and Governments from finding a way to preserve the divisions and closures that the four freedoms are designed to eliminate. In other words, the Treaty and also the Commission's aim was to prevent that the successes obtained could be annihilated by strategic action undertaken, by special interest groups or by national interests.

It cannot be said therefore, that it is by mere coincidence that the Community system, taken as a whole, has deliberately conferred on the Commission the task of guiding the market liberalisation process, but rather that there are precise reasons underlying this structure. Thus, it is with the necessary support supplied by the case-law of the Court of Justice that the Commission has provided a general and sufficiently sound reference framework for all Member States, enhancing to their utmost the potentials of the rules of the Treaty and materialising its main ideas.

This framework has been affected by the increase in the number of Member States of the Community and also by an increased awareness of competition issues by undertakings, to the point of compromising the Commission's capability to deal effectively with the monitoring demands placed upon it. At the same time Member States have gained substantial ground in terms of harmonising industrial policy with the more recent liberalisation trends, adopting specific legislative instruments and creating supervisory bodies, characterised by different degrees of autonomy, in line with DG Competition itself.

The demand for uniformity in safeguarding and promoting competition within the Community, which was met initially by centralising the administrative and jurisdictional regulatory and enforcement powers, has in recent times been satisfied by implementing alternative solutions. Numerous are the factors to be taken into account: consolidated competition policy of the Commission; case-law of the Court and Court of First Instance (CFI), especially with regard to preliminary reference by national judges; the direct effect of Arts. 81(1) and 82 of the Treaty, and hence the wide-ranging application of these rules by national judges and administrative bodies; the introduction of domestic legislative provisions consistent with Community rules, with the attribution to independent authorities of monitoring compliance with the prohibition of unfair competitive practices and, in some States, the expressly attributed power of enforcing Community rules.

There is nothing new or peculiar in the developments mentioned thus far in relation to the manner in which an integrated system like the Community exists and operates. Indeed, there are many Community provisions whose application is not entrusted solely to Community institutions but also or only to national bodies and courts, the latter being emblematically defined as common or natural judges of Community law. This is even more evident when we deal with specific Treaty provisions or Regulations, which often have direct effect, as is the case of most rules on competition: Arts. 81(1) and 82 of the Treaty, Regulation 17/62, and the regulations on block exemptions.

All this has progressively led to a common approach to competition issues and problems in the application of national and Community laws, by the Community and national institutions, be they administrative or judicial. The evolution of the relationship between 'Community' and 'national' safeguard of competition objectives has reduced the relevance of the issue of harmonisation, and has ended up weakening the very concept of 'barrier', replacing it with the usual forms of co-operation, integration, and, stretching the idea somewhat further, subsidiarity, that has always characterised the Community's experience. One might say that this has been a long and constant process of *Communitarisation* of competition law and of a parallel, but directly proportionate process of decentralisation of monitoring and regulation activity of the more important matters. It goes without saying that this process has concerned competition issues related mainly to the conduct of undertakings, and less so the issue of the effects that the conduct of Governments have on competition, for which the Commission appears to be better placed and equipped to compel the Member States to put an end to the infringement of competition, and not only in a pedagogical way.

The main steps in this ongoing process are the following:

(a)  the harmonisation of the national regulations introduced to safeguard competition;
(b)  the direct application of Arts. 81(1) and 82 of the Treaty by the national authorities;
(c)  the institutional co-operation between the Commission and the national authorities in the application of the Community competition rules;
(d)  the idea of decentralising the implementation of Art. 81(3) of the Treaty.


## II


It is a fact that in most States, member of the Community, the content and scope of the national legislations drawn up to protect competition and the market are in line with Community provisions. The process which has led to this situation has been a natural one, since it is not conceivable that the national dimension of any given matter, for instance an agreement capable of affecting trade, could justify a regulation that were to be substantially different from the provisions governing a supranational matter. On the other hand, a competition-oriented culture has taken shape and become consolidated in many Member States under the thrust of the enforcement of Community regulations by the Commission and even more so by the CFI and the Court of Justice, and also as a result of the direct application of most of the provisions by national judges. The States whose legislation is still not in line with the Community legislation are very few and in any case such States do not seem to raise specific problems in terms of harmony of approach and/or regulation.

It is also true that the purely domestic dimension of a case and the Community dimension are interdependent. This quite evidently entails problems of procedural coordination, in particular when there is a risk of parallel procedures which may lead to different outcomes. This, however, reveals also the need for substantial harmonisation of the principles used in approaching a concrete case and its assessment on economic and juridical basis, for example with regards to issues such as market definition and the imposition of fines. From this standpoint, albeit with some doubts as to its juridical foundation, the solution adopted by the Court in the decision on the Oscar Bronner[1] case can be viewed positively. Indeed, in light of the interdependence between community and national legislation on competition matters and in

---

1  Case  C-7/97 (1998) ECR I-7791, Items 12–22.

order to ensure a uniform application of such norms, the Court ruled on a question raised by an Austrian judge dealing with the interpretation of Art. 82 of the Treaty, even though the case concerned a purely domestic controversy where the applicable rule (applied by the competent Competition Authority) was not Art. 82 but the corresponding national rule on the prohibition of abuse of a dominant position.

The progressive and increasingly widespread harmonisation of national legislation with the Community model has also allowed to reduce to a minimum the possibility of conflicts arising from the parallel application of Community and domestic laws, conflicts which the Wilhelm case had resolved, but only partially, on the basis of the principle that of Community Law prevails.[2] This means that a national decision which was found to be inconsistent with the conclusion reached by the Commission following a Community proceeding, must be disregarded; and that the national supervisory authority must 'take appropriate measures' when there are reasons to believe that a divergent decision may be reached by the Commission.[3]

In concrete terms, if an agreement or a concerted practice which have distorting effects on competition are deemed to be consistent with Community Law (Art. 81(1)), in so much as they do not affect infra-Community trade, the national authority could nonetheless legitimately identify a conflict with the municipal structure of competition. On the contrary, if the Commission recognises that the agreement or practice falls within its scope and that they are inconsistent with Art. 81(1), the exemption, if any, envisaged under Art. 81(3), for the application of which the Commission enjoys exclusive competence, precludes the national authority from declaring such agreement or practice in breach of national law. Otherwise, the same agreement could be treated differently depending on the legislative framework of each Member State, and this could thus generate the risk of endangering the uniform application of Community Law. Moreover, this would also mean that the Community exemption provision would not be applied uniformly, thus undermining its full efficacy.

The same holds good in the case of block exemptions which are dealt with by *ad hoc* regulations. In such cases, since it is impossible to adopt decisions which are inconsistent with the regulation itself, the national judge cannot find an agreement or practice, covered by exemption, as being in breach of national competition law; at the most, the national judge can refer the case to the Court in order to obtain a preliminary ruling on the matter, and/or the Commission for relevant information.

## III

With a view to attaining a progressive decentralisation, another very important step is the possibility for the national competition authorities to apply directly Arts. 81(1) and 82 of the Treaty. The position of the Commission has always been that such a possibility was to be ruled out unless specifically envisaged by an *ad hoc* national provision. Consequently, the national authorities would be entitled to doing

---

2 Judgment of 13 February (1969) 14/68, ECR 1.

3 See the Wilhelm judgment, mentioned above, Items 8–9. See also the Judgment of 10 July 1980, Giry and Guerlain, 253/78 and 1-3/79, dealt with together, ECR, p. 2327, Items 15–19. Cases 253/78 and 1-3/79 Giry and Guerlain (1980) ECR 2327, paras 15–19.

this only in the Member States which have already made a provision for the direct application of Community provisions.

At a first analysis this position might appear debatable, and is all the more so when compared with the general principle governing the application of Community rules by the national administrative bodies and judges. One might ask, for instance, why an *ad hoc* eligibility is required when numerous Community rules of the Treaty, as well as various Regulations, are directly applicable by national judges and administrative departments alike (undoubtedly Arts. 81(1) and 82 of the Treaty fall in this category).

Now, strictly speaking, one can share the idea according to which, where Community rules endowed with direct effect are involved, national judges and administrative bodies can or rather must apply them. This is to be taken to mean, according to the well known scheme, that in case of conflict between national and Community rule, the former prevails over the latter. Now, this raises no special problems, and less so for the judge who has an instrument for further exploration, that is the preliminary reference under Art. 234 (ex Art. 177). On the other hand, Community Law itself confers the power on national authorities to apply Arts. 81(1) and 82 of the Treaty, albeit subjecting the exercise of such power to the condition that the Commission has not already started any formal procedure on the same facts.[4]

It is true that with respect to the typical model of Community rules endowed with direct effect, Arts. 81(1) and 82 of the Treaty are characterised by a peculiar trait that requires further reflection. Important investigative and evaluation activities are required in cases of agreements capable of affecting trade and abusive practices of a dominant position. Such a complex task, though it can be attributed to a national judge, with regards to the analysis of the legal questions, who in any case can always ask for a preliminary ruling from the Court of Justice, might also be attributed, albeit with more hesitation, to a national administration whose responsibilities did not specifically include competition matters.

This leads me to the consideration that, especially where there is an *ad hoc* national body designed to ensure compliance with the rules on competition, there should be no hesitation in considering it eligible for applying Community provisions on competition endowed with direct effect, irrespective of the recognition or not of any *ad hoc* eligibility. This is all the more true if, as in many countries, the domestic laws are shaped in perfect accordance with the Community provisions and even impose the constraint that the interpretation of national provisions must be consistent with Community practice and case-law.

In any case, intellectual exercises aside, one should favourably view the fact that in as many as eight States the competition authorities have been formally endowed with competence to apply directly Arts. 81(1) and 82 of the Treaty.[5] Such competence takes on special importance even in cases in which the national competition law is in accordance with Community provisions, precisely because it allows the national authority to apply directly the Community rule as it is normally interpreted

---

4 See, in particular, Art. 9(3) of Regulation no. 17/62; as well as the Judgment of 30 January 1974, 127/73, BRT/SABAM, ECR, p. 51. Case 127/73 BRT/SABAM, (1974) ECR 51.

5 In Italy this competence has been attributed to the Antitrust Authority by Art. 54 of Community Act no. 94 of 1996.

and applied by the Community Institutions. This is no little accomplishment. Indeed, while the finding that an agreement is in breach of competition under Art. 81 or under the corresponding national Act may not entail any difference in consequences, much broader horizons would be opened-up for the national authorities in the case in which, consistently with a now well-consolidated case-law of the Court of Justice,[6] they were to apply Art. 81 in conjunction with Arts. 3 and 5, now 10, of the same Treaty. Indeed, according to this case-law, a national legislation or government that gives incentives to an agreement, encourages it or allows it to consolidate, could be incompatible with the rules of competition law, and for this reason disapplied: something that is absolutely precluded by applying only the domestic antitrust rules.

# IV

Another important step in the evolution of the relationship between the Commission and the national competition authorities is the Notice of October 1997 on the decentralised application of Community competition rules. The aim of this Notice, adopted after a long and a thorough fruitful exchange of views by DGIV and the national authorities, was to encourage a more widespread and efficient application of Arts. 81(1) and 82 of the Treaty at the domestic level and rationalise and regulate co-operation with the national authorities in matters which fall under the scope of Community Law.

As a matter of principle, a criterion which is very close to subsidiarity is set forth. Since the aim of the entire Community system is to adopt decisions at a level that come as close as possible to the citizens, the decentralised application of Community competition provisions enables the Commission to intervene only if, 'by reason of its scale or effects, the proposed action can best be taken at Community level. Otherwise, it is for the competition authority of the Member State concerned to act' (Item 2). The aims pursued are the following:

(a) to ensure greater efficiency in applying competition rules, with a view to also developing and consolidating the single market, by strengthening the role of the national competition authorities, that are closer to the markets and to the undertakings involved, and are therefore in a better position than the Commission to detect anti-competitive behaviour producing national effects (Items 6 and 12);
(b) to define the principles that the Commission intends to follow in dealing with matters which are important for co-operation and which prompt undertakings to address the national competition authorities more frequently;
(c) to take action so that the matters falling within the scope of Community Law are dealt with by a single authority, also to avoid among other things *forum shopping* practices.

---

6 See, for instance, Judgment of 17 November 1993, C-2/91, Meng., ECR I-5791, and Judgment of 16 November 1977, 13/77, Inno/ATAB, ECR 2115; as well as Judgment of 18 June 1998, 35/96, Commission/Italy, Case 35/96 Commission v. Italy (1998) ECR 3851; Case C-2/91 Criminal Proceedings against Meng (1993) I-5751; Case 13/77 Inno/ATAB (1977) 2115.

There is a clear concern to reduce to a minimum the negative consequences of some national authorities not having been recognised as eligible to apply Arts. 81 and 82. The invitation asking Member Countries that have not yet done so, to confer this power on their national competition authorities is to be viewed in this perspective (Item 65); the same holds good for the invitation by the Commission to the national authorities, which have been enabled to do so, to effectively apply the Community rules (Item 15) and to do so in such a way as to meet the need for a uniform application of Community law throughout the Community and for the respect of the principle of good faith co-operation as laid down in Art. 5 (now Art. 10) of the Treaty (Item 16). Ultimately, there is a concern about conflicts between decisions adopted on the basis of Community Law and those adopted in accordance with domestic law.

This concern emerges even more clearly in the specific guidelines aimed at settling the conflicts between the decisions of the Commission and subsequent decisions taken by national authorities in the 'same case'. According to the Commission, when a national authority applies Community law it should comply with the decision taken by the Commission; and in the case of a position expressed through a comfort letter, the opinion expressed therein constitutes a factor that should be taken into account (Item 17).

A problematic aspect concerns the relationship between a decision adopted by a national authority based on national law and the Commission's decision. Where an infringement of Arts. 81(1) and 82 of the Treaty is established by a Commission decision, the national authority is not entitled to issue a ruling which is, in any respect, less stringent, given the supremacy of Community law and the need for its uniform application (Item 18). This, as mentioned earlier, is in my opinion clear and unquestionable.

As to the opposite case, where national authorities may apply a more stringent national competition law to a matter which has previously been the subject of an individual exemption decision by the Commission or which is covered by a block exemption Regulation, the Notice states that 'The legal position is less clear' (Item 19). It does, however, make a general reference to the Wilhelm case and to the opinion presented by the advocate general in the Volkswagen[7] case, reconfirming the need to apply Community law uniformly and the need for decisions pursuant to Art. 81(3) to be effective.

As pointed out earlier, since the agreements in question may affect trade between Member States and hence fall under the scope of Art. 81(1) of the Treaty, the existence of an individual exemption compels national authorities to 'accept' the positive assessment made by the Commission. If this were not the case, not only could the same agreement be evaluated differently in each Member State, thus undermining the uniform application of Community Law, but this would also result in denying full effectiveness of a Community decision, in this case an exemption granted on the basis of Art. 81(3), which should produce identical effects in all Member States. Moreover, the application of block exemption Regulations leads to precisely the same conclusions. Indeed, these are directly effective rules, and as such are binding

---

7 Judgment of 24 October 1995, C-266/93, ECR, I-3477. Case 266/93 Volkswagen (1995) ECR I-3477.

on a national judge, in so far as no decision can be made which is incompatible. In other words, a judge cannot apply the regulation to agreements which are not covered by the exemption, or *vice versa* not apply the exemption to agreements which are included, retaining, of course, the possibility of referring the matter to the Court.

The criteria utilised for allocating cases between the Commission and national authorities are three. The first has to do with the effects of the agreement or of the abuse, namely that national authorities will handle cases whose effects are felt mainly in the market corresponding to the territory of a single Member State (Items 26–28). The second criterion concerns the nature of the infringement (Items 29–32), according to which national authorities cannot deal with cases already notified to the Commission in order to obtain an exemption in accordance with Art. 81(3), nor with cases where the decision to be taken is whether to withdraw an exemption previously granted. The third criterion concerns cases of particular interest for the Community (Items 33–36), for which there is normally more margin for discretion. In particular, this category includes cases which raise a new point of law, that is to say, those which have not yet been the subject of a Commission decision or a judgement of the CFI or the Court; cases of special economic importance; and finally, cases in which exclusive rights have been granted, more generally the cases which fall within the scope of application of Art. 86 (ex Art. 90). On the other hand, the Notice underlines the need for the action of the national authority to be effective from the standpoint also of investigative powers, which are linked to the size of national territory; it also emphasises the need for the national body to be able to adopt interim measures in a case of urgency, and to have the power of imposing fines on the undertakings found guilty of infringing the competition rules; finally, there have to be suitable procedural rules which ensure uniformity of treatment when similar cases are dealt with.

With regard to cases falling within the scope of Community law, which have been brought before a national authority, the Notice suggests, as a first point, that the national authorities should systematically inform the Commission of any such proceedings that have been initiated. This is particularly important for cases which are of special interest for the Community. The procedure is the one established by national law and the national authorities can address the Commission for any information they may need; the Commission has to offer close co-operation so as to eliminate the risk of conflicting decisions.

The Notice does envisage the risk of contradictory decisions in the case of parallel procedures: the national authority will have to take the necessary measures to ensure full efficacy of the actions taken in enforcing Community competition law. There is an alternative. The first branch is to temporarily suspend the national procedure pending the outcome of the proceedings conducted by the Commission; in practice since the time frames of the Commission are not at all brief, this would be a *sine die* interruption.

This solution could create problems, and as such could ultimately prompt unwillingness to directly apply Community rules by national authorities. The second branch of the alternative is that the Commission should consult with the national authority before issuing its final decision. This would involve an exchange of documents and would ensure that the national authorities could keep track of the Commission's position without having to wait for its final decision.

## V

The right to grant exemptions has so far been considered by the Commission as being its exclusive prerogative. Under Regulation 17 this has been up to now a 'natural monopoly'. In the last few years there has been talk, which has progressively gained in volume, concerning the possibility of enabling the Member States also to apply Art. 81(3) in order to allocate responsibilities between the Commission and national competition authorities, either on the basis of the centre of gravity of the cases, or on the basis of turnover thresholds, along the lines of Regulation (EEC) no. 4064/89. Such idea which aims at realising a full and complete decentralisation, and which is part of a broader 'modernisation' project of the rules for the application of Arts. 81 and 82, has arisen first as an answer to a need that has become increasingly stronger, from the moment national authorities were expressly recognised as having the power of directly applying Arts. 81(1) and 82.

At the present time, indeed, full application of such rules does not occur, also because the national authorities sometimes fear that their action may be blocked by a strategic action undertaken by the parties involved. Such a preemptive action may consist in filing a request for an exemption with Brussels—and this because the possibility of granting an exemption under Art. 81(3) continues to be an exclusive power of the Commission. In this connection, it must be said that the mechanism referred by the Commission in point 57 of the Notice on co-operation with national competition authorities in order to avoid dilatory notifications, i.e. notifications aimed to thwart the actions of the body to which the matter has been referred, have not encountered with the success expected.

Secondly, the decentralisation effort is also motivated by the need to expand the resources utilised to enforce Community rules, given the growing difficulties encountered by the Commission, in terms of resources, in carrying out the extensive caseload resulting from the notification system.

With regard to this latter remark, it goes without saying that the advantages of the so-called modernisation would be important, precisely because the Commission could concentrate on cases of greater importance and on those for which its action would be more effective than that of the national authorities. This in turn would enable the Commission to concentrate on ensuring fair competition in trans-national agreements and on maintaining a market structure based on fair competition.

A fundamental step in this direction has been made with the 'White Paper on the Modernisation of the rules implementing Arts. 85 and 86 (now 81 and 82) of the EC Treaty'.[8] The Commission's proposed reform amounts to a sweeping revision of Regulation 17 and, in particular, it turns upside down the current system for the application of Art. 81 of the EC Treaty. In fact, after discussing several options for reform, the White Paper proposes the abolition of the notification and exemption system and its replacement by a new regulation which would render the exemption rule of Art. 81(3) directly applicable without prior decision by the Commission. It follows that Art. 81 as a whole would be applied by the Commission, national competition authorities and national courts, as is already the case for Arts. 81(1) and 82.

---

8 The *White Paper* has been approved by the Commission on 28 April 1999 (OJ C132 of 12 May 1999).

This departure from the existing authorisation system, in which the Art. 81 prohibition can be waived only by an act of a public authority empowered to do so to a directly applicable exception system, whereby agreements that meet certain criteria specified by law are outside the scope of the prohibition contained in Art. 81, represents a very radical reform, involving a complete abandonment of the prior control and administrative exemption decisions for all the agreements which fall under Art. 81(1). Therefore, it goes further than the ongoing debate as to whether or not the application of Art. 81(3) could ever be entrusted to national competition authorities. Adopting a directly applicable exception system and *ex post* abuse control means, actually, not only removing the exclusive power conferred on the Commission as regards the application of Art. 81(3), but also that the undertakings would have to make their own assessment of the compatibility with Community law of their restrictive practices, in the light of course of the legislation in force and the relevant case-law. The White Paper suggests to maintain the system of compulsory prior notification only as far as 'partial-function production' joint ventures are concerned: the prior authorisation requirement appears desirable in this case, taking into account that operations of this kind require substantial investment and wide integration of operations, which normally makes it difficult to unravel them afterwards.

In any case, a decentralised application of the competition rules would be facilitated, because any administrative authority or court endowed with the necessary powers could carry out a full assessment of restrictive practices referred to it, examining both their restrictive effects under Art. 81(1) and any economic benefits under Art. 81(3).

Practical objections have been levelled against this proposal, in particular as to how to counter the danger of diverging interpretation by different authorities, courts and self-assessing undertakings: I cannot share such concerns. I think that, first of all, the assessment by the national authorities of agreement or abuse of dominant position is in actual fact only one aspect of decentralisation as foreshadowed in its essential and exhaustive traits already in the 1957 Treaty. National judges and administrative agencies are indeed the main actors in the application of all Community rules: and the competition rules are not an exception. For instance, suffice it to mention Art. 28 (ex Art. 30), along with Art. 30 (ex Art. 36), and again the exceptions that have been exposed by the case-law as being inherent in Art. 28 itself. Upon close consideration these provisions have been applied without any problems by national judges and administrative bodies. They have raised the issue of uniform application, but the important case-law on this issue is sufficient for guaranteeing that differences in application are the exception and not the rule. There is no reason, therefore, to be apprehensive about of decentralising the application of Art. 81(3), since this is a rule like the others. Hence both national judges and national administrations, and in particular the competition authorities, may enforce it appropriately.

Besides all this, the reform would in any case recognise the Commission as having a prominent role in shaping the Community competition policy. In this connection it is worth noting that the White Paper points out the Commission's intention to adopt block exemption regulation with a wider scope of application, using market share thresholds to cover the vast majority of agreements, in particular those concluded by small and medium-sized undertakings. It also intends to draw up more notices and guidelines to explain and expound its policy and provide guidance for the application of the competition rules by national bodies. Furthermore, even within the new framework, the Commission intends to adopt, in exceptional cases, individual decisions, which are not prohibition decisions of a declaratory nature, to provide the market with guidance in relation to the Commission's approach to certain restrictions. Moreover, the White Paper also points out the Commission's intention to introduce a new kind of individual decision, in which it would take note of the commitments entered into by the parties in the course of the proceedings that might otherwise end with a prohibition and render them binding.

Moreover, in a system of multiple competence of the Commission, national and judicial authorities, protection mechanisms are, in any case, envisaged. I am referring in particular to the possibility that the Commission may reserve for itself the right to deal with a particular case and order that a pending case before the national authorities be deferred to it, and also the duty incumbent upon national authorities and judges not to adopt decisions inconsistent with those of the Commission.

Ultimately, I do not believe that the concerns regarding the decentralisation of the application of Art. 81(3) are legitimate or that they rest on valid grounds. Quite the contrary, it is true that such a reform, with the necessary adjustments, could and should be such as to enable a greater uniformity of application of Community competition law because the very same provisions, and not 15 different national legislations, would be applied in all Member States. If any, the problem lies elsewhere, and is essentially organisational in character. An effective and thorough decentralisation necessarily requires a strengthening of co-operation and of the circulation of information not only between Member States and the Commission, but also among the national authorities themselves. This is where efforts should be focused. In this respect the proposal referred to in the White Paper of convening the Advisory Committee to deal with a particular case examined by a national authority in application of Arts. 81 and 82 of the Treaty is particularly welcome. It appears to be a useful tool of solving possible conflicts in interpretation. An idea that could also solve some of the problems at least is to set up a sort of 'Brussels' Convention on Competition, whereas to solve *all* of the problems time is needed, as has occurred in other area and rules of Community law. In this connection it is worth noting that an important instrument of co-operation among competition authorities consists in sharing informations provided to them in connection with competition procedures. However, according to the Court of Justice[9] the competition authorities of the Member States are not permitted to make use, for the purposes of the application of Arts. 81 and 82, of information provided to them by the Commission which the Commission has obtained in answer to a request pursuant to Art. 11 of Regulation 17 or in an application for negative clearance or exemption. A similar prohibition of disclosure of information or data regarding an undertaking involved in a formal investigation by the national competition authority is provided for in most of the legislation of the Member States. It follows that in order to strengthen the co-operation mechanisms among the competition authorities, this legislation would have to be amended with the aim to entitle this exchange of information, with the

---

9 Case C-67/91 *Dirección General de la Defensa de la Competencia* v. *AEBP*, judgement of 16 July 1992, (1992) ECR I-1475.

limitation, however, as the Commission suggests in the White Paper, that the information could be used only for the purpose for which it was originally gathered and for the application of Arts. 81 and 82 or for national competition law. I think that is a basic issue.

To sum up, I have no doubt that we can and must devise a system which reconciles the objective of effective decentralisation with a rigorous and uniform application of Community competition law throughout the Member States.

# Chapter Two: Decentralised Application of Community Competition Law

## JOHN TEMPLE-LANG[1]

Decentralisation of the application of Community competition law is now possible because in the last few years, a majority of Member States have set up effective competition authorities and have national competition laws based on Community rules. These authorities at least are in a position to carry out the original intention of the EC Treaty, that Community competition law should be applied partly by national authorities. All national competition authorities now have a clearer understanding of their duties to co-operate with the Commission under Art. 5 (now 10) EC Treaty,[2] and the Commission's reciprocal duty to help them to apply Community competition law. There is now a large body of case-law of the Community courts and many decisions of the Commission so that the legal principles which national courts and competition authorities should apply are reasonably clear. The case-law will increase greatly as national competition authorities apply national laws similar to Community competition rules, and the Court of Justice will advise on Community law issues even if it is national law which is being applied.[3] The Commission is adopting guidelines and group exemptions, which should clarify the legal position in many common situations: in most cases the main task of national courts and authorities is to find and assess the facts.

Decentralisation is desirable because national competition authorities, if they are reasonably effective, can apply national and Community competition rules simultaneously, largely avoiding questions about effects on trade between Member States. They can operate in one language, and they should know their national markets better than the Commission could. Many competition cases involve companies in the same Member State and need little evidence, which is outside the jurisdiction and beyond the reach of discovery orders or the equivalent. The principle of subsidiarity says that cases should be dealt with at the level nearest to the citizen at which they can be dealt with satisfactorily. National courts, if they were free to apply Art. 85(3) (now 81(3)) could do so in cases in which they could award compensation or issue injunctions or declarations. Decentralisation is needed to avoid, as far as possible, multiple procedures in same situations.

---

1 A Director in the Directorate General for Competition, European Commission; Professor, Trinity College, Dublin; Senior Visiting Research Fellow, University of Oxford; Barrister. All opinions expressed are purely personal.
2 Temple-Lang, The Core of the Constitutional Law of the Community—Art. 5 EC, in Gormley (Ed.), Current and Future Perspectives on EC Competition Law (Kluwer, 1997), pp. 41–72.
3 Case C-28/95, Leur-Bloem, 1997 ECR I 4161. Case C-7/97, Oscar Bronner, (1998) ECR I-7791.

*J. Rivas and M. Horspool (eds), Modernisation and Decentralisation of EC Competition Law*, 13–29.
© 2000 *Kluwer Law International.*

Decentralisation is also necessary. This is because the number of cases brought before the Commission and the elaborate procedures imposed by Reg. 17 make it impossible for the Commission to deal with them all by formal decisions. This situation, unless radically dealt with, will get worse when the Community is enlarged by the accession of an additional five, ten or more Member States in the next few years. Approximately 60% of all cases are brought before the Commission by notification, and most others by complaints. The most serious infringements are not being detected quickly enough or often enough, and they are never notified in practice, since they would have no chance of being approved. Practices of dominant companies which may be prohibited by Art. 86 (now 82) are never notified and even companies which are aware of them are often reluctant to complain, for fear of reprisals. The Commission needs to rid itself of unnecessary notifications so that it can concentrate on the most serious horizontal cartels and the most serious violations of Art. 86 (now 82).

## I. Objectives

The Commission has therefore proposed several objectives. The most important of those which concern national competition authorities and courts directly, with which this paper is primarily concerned, is to enable them both to apply Art. 85(3). To enable courts to do this, Art. 85(3) must be treated as a provision which is directly applicable without any previous administrative authorisation, reversing the choice which was made in 1962 when Reg. 17 was adopted. This also enables the Commission to dispense with notifications (except in state aids and merger Regulation cases). These changes lead to the need for arrangements, discussed below, for allocation of cases between the Commission and national competition authorities, for effective co-ordination, and other consequential arrangements. These consequential arrangements include ensuring that multiple procedures by different national authorities and courts are avoided as far as possible and that there is effective judicial review of all substantive decisions of national competition authorities. In addition, as a counterpart to more generous group exemptions, and recognising that in an enlarged Community circumstances in national markets may differ substantially, the Commission has suggested that national competition authorities should have power to withdraw the benefit of group exemptions in their Member States.

## II. The main changes in Commission procedures

This paper concentrates on the implications of the Commission's proposals[4] for national authorities and courts, but it is essential to summarise the proposals insofar as they concern the Commission itself. The main change is that notifications will no

---

4 European Commission, White Paper on Modernisation of the rules implementing Arts. 85 and 86 of the EC Treaty, OJ no. C-132/1, 12 May 1999: Schaub, EC Competition System—proposals for reform, 22 Fordham International Law Journal (1999), pp. 853–884.

longer be made under what is now Reg. 17. The scope of the Merger Regulation may be slightly extended. If agreements are brought to the Commission's attention, it will have no obligation to express a view on them, and any views which it expresses will be declaratory and not constitutive. However, the Commission will have a new power to adopt decisions approving agreements on the basis of commitments made by the parties, making the commitments legally binding on the parties and enforceable by third parties.

In addition, it is intended to formalise and simplify procedures in interim measures cases, to provide for judicial approval of surprise inspections, and to give the Commission increased powers to question individual witnesses. The fines for misleading and incomplete information will be increased, and also the daily payments made to enforce Commission orders.

## III. Strengthening national competition authorities

These proposals make it desirable, and in some Member States necessary, to strengthen the national competition authorities. There seem to be five main requirements for effective national competition authorities:[5]

—they must have express power to apply Community competition law, and they must have express powers to impose fines and to make all other orders needed to ensure that Community competition rules are fully and effectively enforced;
—they must have enough staff to handle their workloads efficiently;
—they must have procedures, which enable them to decide cases in a reasonable time;
—they must have, and be seen to have, sufficient independence, professionalism and objectivity to inspire the confidence of the companies appearing before them;
—they must have powers and procedures which enable them to enforce the law, when necessary, quickly and effectively. This means that they must have adequate powers to get evidence, to question witnesses, to order interim measures, and so on. This does *not* mean that in each Member State there must necessarily be an administrative authority with power to fine or to impose penalties or prohibit specific conduct. If national constitutional law prohibits this, or if it is thought better that such powers should be exercised only by courts, it is perfectly satisfactory for enforcement measures to be taken by courts, provided that the courts have all the necessary standing and powers for effective enforcement.

---

5 Commission Notice on co-operation between national competition authorities and the Commission, OJ no. C-313/3, 15 October 1997. See Temple-Lang, General Report on national application of European competition law, in XVIII Congress of the Fédération Internationale pour le Droit Européen (Stockholm 1998), vols. II and IV: Temple-Lang, European Community constitutional law and the enforcement of Community antitrust law in Hawk (Ed.), 1993 Fordham Corporate Law Institute (1994), pp. 525–604.

In other words, national competition authorities may need more money, more staff, greater legal powers, or a greater degree of independence, whether from industry or from government.

In addition, some obstacles to effective enforcement by national competition authorities may have to be removed by legislation, either at national or Community level. One obstacle results from the Spanish Banks judgement,[6] which ruled, in effect, that evidence obtained by the Commission could not be used by national authorities even to apply Community law. This obstacle could be removed only by Community legislation.

On the other hand, there are a number of obstacles to action by national authorities which result from national legislation exempting certain sectors from their jurisdiction, or providing that they may not take any action against State-owned companies. All of these should be repealed before the competition authorities in the Member States in question can be fully effective. In addition, there are various weaknesses, perhaps falling short of real obstacles, which probably should be corrected by appropriate national legislation.

At present, national competition authorities have a duty not to approve any practice, or any price resulting from a practice, which is contrary to Community competition law.[7] It is important to ensure that this principle is respected more fully in future, especially as national authorities will have power to apply Art. 85(3). This principle means that an approval given by a national competition authority (or of course a national regulatory authority) can be challenged in national courts on the ground that it approves something prohibited by Community competition law.

Although the Commission's proposals do not include or envisage any harmonisation of the procedures of national competition authorities, other than those implicit in ensuring that the authorities are able to apply Community law effectively, one issue which is likely to arise is the rights of complainants to get rulings in their complaints. It would presumably be important that these should be similar in all national laws, and similar to the rights of complainants before the Commission. If they were not, forum shopping would be inevitable.

Another change concerns co-operation between national competition authorities. At present almost all of them are prohibited from giving confidential information to any other competition authority, including the Commission, even to enable the receiving authority to apply Community competition law. It will be necessary, if any system for rational allocation of cases between European competition authorities is to work, to authorise exchanges of otherwise confidential information for Community law enforcement.

All of these steps to increase the powers and effectiveness of national competition authorities, and in particular the principle of allocating Community competition cases between competition authorities, necessarily means that national authorities will at least in some circumstances have a duty (and not merely a power) to apply Community competition law. This duty would arise under Art. 5 (now 10) EC Treaty. Presumably it would not be stricter than that imposed

---

6 Case C-67/91, Asociación Española de Banca Privada, 1992 ECR I 4785.
7 Case 209-213/84, Asjes 1986 ECR 1425: Case 66/86, Ahmed Saeed, 1989 ECR 803.

on the Commission, *mutatis mutandis*: the Commission is not legally obliged to investigate every complaint exhaustively. But the qualification indicated by the Latin phrase is important. Neither the Commission nor a national authority is obliged by Community law to investigate a complaint further than it thinks necessary in order to arrive at a conclusion on the merits of the complaint. But the Commission, unlike a national authority, can say, if appropriate, that it does not need to investigate a complaint because even if it is entirely justified it could satisfactorily be dealt with at national level, either by the competition authority or by the courts, and the interests of the Community do not require Commission intervention.

However difficult it may be to assess the existing national authorities in terms of their independence, efficiency, professionalism and objectivity, continued efforts to do so must be made. A useful precedent for this type of assessment is already being carried out under the Telecommunications directives which require national telecommunications regulators to be independent from both the national telecommunications company and the Ministry responsible for telecommunications policy. Both the Commission and companies will have to have confidence in national competition authorities in all respects if decentralisation is to work well. The improvements which are undoubtedly necessary do not all have to be made before the Commission's proposals come into force, but equally they cannot be made over night. Much depends on the integrity and independence of character of the heads of the competition authorities. But, if assessments are to be made, factual questions could be asked about the professional and academic qualifications and experience of the staff, whether they are on secondment from the national civil service or from private industry, whether they are permanent or temporary, how many of them there are, how many cases there are per staff member, and so on.

Strengthening national competition authorities also means closer links between them, so that they can share analysis and discuss problems as well as sharing evidence. This means among other things, making available decisions of national authorities on their websites and providing summaries in other languages. If important decisions of national authorities are discussed between them and with the Commission, with the aim of reaching the same result whichever authority handles the case, the weight of the decision of whichever authority decides will be increased.

However, until the independence of each national authority is established beyond question, doubts may arise when a national authority deals with a complaint against a State-owned enterprise. It might be useful for all such cases to be discussed by the national authority concerned with the Commission, and for this practice to be made known.


## IV. Increasing national courts' powers

The Commission's proposals, if carried out substantially as suggested in the White Paper, will have a number of consequences for national courts.

Most obviously, they will have power to apply Art. 85(3), without any previous decision by any administrative authority. They will do this, subject to any new measures which may be thought necessary, and to any general duties under

Community law (Art. 5 EC, now Art. 10[8]) which may be relevant in any particular case, in accordance with their normal national rules of procedure and evidence. Essentially, two kinds of cases are involved: commercial disputes between private parties (or between a private party and a State-owned enterprise) in which the lawfulness of a contract or practice is in dispute, and judicial review of the decisions of national competition authorities. National courts already are obliged to give effective protection for rights given by Community law, in particular by giving injunctions, compensation, or declaring clauses in contracts to be invalid. In any claim for these kinds of relief the court may need to decide whether a given clause in contrary to Art. 85, and for this purpose to apply Art. 85(3).

If national competition authorities are to apply Community law more often and in more important cases, it is essential that their decisions must be subject to effective judicial review. This is necessary to protect the rights of the parties, and also the rights of complainants: some clarification of complainants' rights to appeal against rejections of complaints by national competition authorities will probably be needed. It is also necessary because in most Member States competition decisions are taken in the first instance by a body which is not a tribunal within the meaning of Art. 177 (now 234). To make sure that uniform application of Community competition law can be ensured, as far as necessary, it is essential that judicial review (or an appeal) considers the merits sufficiently to allow any issue of Community law to be referred to the Court of Justice. Judicial review on procedural grounds only would not be sufficient (and might even be a violation of the duty of the courts under Art. 10 to provide effective protection of substantive Community law rights). There may be questions about the extent to which judicial review or appeals lead in practice to suspension of the decisions on the competition authority: the effective enforcement of Community competition law must not be unduly impeded by suspension of decisions resulting from appeals or judicial review. As already mentioned, it would be a valid ground for annulling a competition authority's decision if it had approved, under national competition law, an agreement or practice, or a price resulting from a practice, which was contrary to Arts. 85–86.[9]

Apart from the question (discussed below) whether national courts may need any help in applying Art. 81, there are several other issues. The national competition authority, or even the European Commission, might be given a right to appeal in the higher national courts against an important judgement of a lower court which they believe to be incorrect. The national competition authority should be informed automatically if a significant issue of Community law arises in court proceedings. There may be a need to harmonise treatment of confidential information in courts and in competition authorities, even within the same State. There may perhaps be a

---

8 Commission Notice on co-operation between national courts and the Commission in applying Arts. 85 and 86, OJ no. C-39/6, 13 February 1993: Temple-Lang, The duties of national courts under Community constitutional law, 22 European Law Review (1997), pp. 3–18: Temple-Lang, Judicial National Attitudes to Community Law and consequences for evolving Community Law, in Sundström and Kauppi, Access to Justice: the Architecture of the European Community Courts (Helsinki 1999), pp. 57–105.

9 Case 66/86, Ahmed Saeed, 1989 ECR 803.

need to clarify the duty of national courts to avoid the risk of conflicts between their judgments and decisions of the Commission (even though the elimination of notifications, and the new power of the courts to apply Art. 85(3), will mean that notifications for purposes of delay should no longer occur).

## V. Allocation of cases

Under the Commission's suggestions, in relation to individual cases the most important difference between the powers of the Commission and the powers of national authorities, as far as Community law is concerned, would be that the jurisdiction of each national authority would be confined to one member State. If therefore a case could only be dealt with by investigating the market or the behaviour of companies in several States, the Commission would need to deal with the case. If however all the parties and all the relevant evidence was in one State, the national authority in that State could, and normally should, handle the case. However, a complainant does not necessarily know whether companies in more than one State are involved in a restrictive agreement, or where the relevant evidence is situated. A complainant is not necessarily in the same State as the companies complained against. Unless it wishes to complain to the Commission for some reason, a complainant may prefer to complain to the competition authority in its own State, if only for linguistic reasons. If a complaint is made to one national authority, that authority may discover that another national authority is already investigating the same agreement or practice, or that some important evidence is in another jurisdiction. A complaint which is made initially to the Commission may prove to be one which could be satisfactorily dealt with by a single national authority. In all situations of these kinds, it may be appropriate to transfer the case from one national authority to another, or between a national authority and the Commission, at the start of the investigation.

Even if the relevant national authority is perfectly capable in theory of handling the case, there may be reasons why it would prefer not to do so. It may be short staffed and overworked. It may have no experience in a technical area. The complaint may be against a State enterprise, and it may be felt that the ultimate decision would inspire more confidence if it was taken by the Commission. The national authority may have some relevant defect in its legal powers which has not yet been corrected by legislation. The authority may know that the Commission is already dealing with similar cases in other Member States, or the Commission may wish to treat the case as a precedent or as a test case. Although the directly relevant evidence is all in one Member State, the case might be more satisfactorily handled if similar situations in other States were also looked at.

Other considerations may arise if there are reasons why the case should also be treated under national law, e.g. because the agreement complained against has already been notified to a national authority under national procedures, or because another similar complaint has already been made to the national authority about the same practice, or because the national authority has withdrawn the benefit of a relevant group exemption from the industry or company in question (if national authorities are given the power to do this).

Several conclusions can be drawn from all this:

—Guidelines for complainants, about which authority to complain to, will be needed.
—Although it is undesirable to transfer cases from one authority to another after a complainant has been received, that may sometimes be worthwhile, for practical reasons.
—A complainant may not always have all the information which would be useful to decide which authority is best placed to deal with the complaint, or the complainant may have some reason to try to complain to another authority.
—The number and variety of considerations which it may be useful to take into account if a complaint is made initially to both the Commission and a national authority is very large. It would be difficult if not impossible to lay down rules covering all, or even a majority, of the situations foreseeable.[10]
—It would *not* be desirable to have rules for allocating cases which were legally binding or which otherwise gave companies opportunities to make preliminary objections to the exercice of jurisdiction by whatever authority was thought appropriate. This would cause delay, unnecessary litigation, and expense, and make application of Community competition law less effective. If the system envisaged by the Commission is fully set up, the final result ought to be the same irrespective of which authority decides the case.
—So it seems that for the immediately foreseeable future informal, pragmatic and non-legally binding arrangements for allocation of cases between the Commission and national authorities would be best, and indeed would be essential. This would mean that the Commission would be entitled, in appropriate cases, to refuse to deal with a complaint on the grounds that it had been agreed for good reasons that it should be handled by a national authority. None of this would, in itself, alter the rights of parties under national law and national procedures. But no doubt national authorities would be even more anxious than they are at present to avoid unnecessary duplication of procedures.
—Non-legally binding guidelines would be useful for the guidance of, and perhaps to reassure, potential complainants. Clearly both the Commission and national authorities should be ready to advise potential complainants which authority their complaints should be sent to. A standard complaint form, even if it was not essential to use it, might be adopted by the Commission and all the national competition authorities. The convenience, linguistic and otherwise, of complainants should be allowed to influence the decision to allocate the case to one authority rather than another. If, while relevant procedural rules remain unharmonised, a complainant has a substantial reason for having its complaint dealt with by one authority rather than another, that reason should be respected unless there is some strong reason for overriding it. The whole system must operate in such a way as to give complainants confidence in it. This may necessitate, among other

---

10 See Temple-Lang, EEC Competition actions in Member States' courts—claims for damages, declarations and injunctions for breach of Community antitrust law, in Henk (Ed.), 1983 Fordham Corporate Law Institute (1994), pp. 219–304, pp. 245–247.

things, some harmonisation of the procedural rights of complainants before national authorities. Complainants will need to be reassured, as far as it is true, that the result should be the same whichever authority handles the case.

However, complainants must accept that if their case is decided by one authority and the result is not to their satisfaction, they cannot complain to another authority and try again: their only remedy is in the administrative courts of the State whose authority decided the case (or in the Court of First Instance, if the case was decided by the Commission). This illustrates why the Commission's proposals may lead ultimately to pressure for some harmonisation of judicial review of decisions of national competition authorities.

—At present not all Member States have equally effective national authorities. It might be right for the Commission to transfer a complaint, in a given set of circumstances, to an efficient national authority, but not to transfer an otherwise similar case to a small, understaffed or ineffective authority, whatever precisely the reasons for its weakness might be. This is a real difficulty which must be recognised. It is yet another reason for having a flexible informal system for allocating cases, since it would be impracticable as well as undiplomatic to have rules which differentiated between national competition authorities by reference to their size or effectiveness. It would be equally impossible to try to distinguish, by rules, between small cases which could be handled satisfactorily by a small authority and large or complex cases which could not.
—One further complication should be mentioned. In some industries, notably telecommunications, there are national regulatory authorities with competition powers as well as national competition authorities. By no means all the issues concerning allocation of cases between regulators and competition authorities, even in the same Member State, have yet been solved. But the Commission already has to decide sometimes whether to deal with a complaint itself or to leave it to a national regulator. If and when the system envisaged by the Commission's White Paper is set up, it will still be necessary to consider whether a complaint would be better dealt with by a national regulatory authority in the industry in question rather than either the Commission or the national competition authority. Since regulators' powers are different from the powers of competition authorities, such a choice raises issues outside the scope of this paper.

### VI. Uniform application of Community competition law and differences of opinion over individual cases

As already mentioned, the ideal to be aimed at is that the result in any given case would be the same whichever competition authority decides it. This is merely another way of saying that Community competition law should be uniformly interpreted and applied throughout the Community. However, it is clear that some arrangements are needed to ensure, as far as reasonably possible, that this ideal is realised in practice. As far as national competition authorities are concerned, this objective can be sought through administrative contacts and co-operation. The difficulty is to ensure a reasonable level of uniformity *without* requiring every formal decision of every national authority to be discussed by the existing Advisory Committee or some similar body. The administrative arrangements most suited to obtaining the balance between simple and speedy procedures and uniform application have yet to be worked out, and primarily concern the competition authorities (including the Commission) rather than practising lawyers. However, several points can be made:

—Cases in civil or commercial courts are decided only between the parties, and on the evidence they have been able to put before the court. Decisions by competition authorities apply *vis-à-vis* all interested parties. Also, the Brussels Convention applies to civil and commercial judgments but not to judgments of administrative courts.

—When different conclusions are reached in competition cases, it is usually due to different views of the facts rather than different view of the law.

—Different conclusions may be reached, and may all be valid, if two authorities are looking at the effects of the same agreement in different markets. The Commission is obliged to look at the whole European market if it is affected by the agreement: a national authority is obliged to consider only its national market. This may well lead to different results.

—It would clearly be desirable to avoid conflicting decisions by two authorities about the same facts. Art. 5 EC (now Art. 10) imposes a general duty on national authorities to avoid any substantial risk of conflict between their decisions and those of the Commission in the same cases. However, if the Commission's present proposals are adopted, national competition authorities will not adopt favourable decisions under Community law, and the scope for conflicting decisions will be very limited. If two decisions *are* necessary and *are* concerned with different markets (or with different but similar facts for some other reason, even if only due to availability of evidence), this should not necessarily give rise to criticism. European industry has lived until now with national competition laws which were very different from one another, and with Community competition rules which were not applied at all in many situations in which they could have been applied. The result has undoubtedly been that the economic results were not uniform throughout Europe, yet no protests were made. It would be unreasonable to insist that the new system envisaged in the White Paper should guarantee uniform results in national competition authority procedures from the start. Industry's need for the quickest and simplest procedures reasonably possible is at least as great as its need for uniform application of Community competition law. Uniform application of *other* rules of Community law by national courts is guaranteed by Art. 177 (now 234).

—The first step in each case is for the authority which has received or initiated the case to let the Commission and other national authorities (or at least those which might be involved, or might wish to be involved) know the essential features of the case. This needs to be done to allocate the case to the appropriate authority. Later in the case it will be necessary, at least in some cases, for the authority concerned to tell the Commission, and any other authority which has expressed an interest in the case, how it intends to decide. Any discussion or disagreement which results will have to be completed within any time limit imposed by national law. If there is a disagreement which cannot be resolved, and if the matter is important enough, the Commission could take over the case.[11] This would solve the problem not because the Commission is infallible, but because all its formal decisions will presumably continue to be discussed by the Advisory Committee, and will certainly continue to be subject to judicial review by the Court of First Instance and ultimately the Court of Justice, so that the disagreement can be authoritatively resolved by the Community Courts if necessary.

—Other more elaborate provisions, apart from intensive administrative co-operation could be envisaged, if necessary. The Commission, and other national authorities, could perhaps be given standing to seek judicial review of a competition authority's decisions in the administrative courts of the Member State in question, though it is doubtful if they would make use of it if the companies concerned did not. The Advisory Committee could always discuss any national authority's decision after it had been adopted, to try to get a consensus on how similar cases should be dealt with in future. If it was worthwhile, the Commission could issue a Notice or amend any relevant group exemption. Divergences of views over principles, if they arose, would have to be resolved by one of these methods. But once a national authority's decision has been taken, the fora for reopening that individual case are the national adminstrative courts, subject to Art. 177 (now 234).

—The Commission is not, and must not allow itself to be treated as, a kind of appeal tribunal from the decisions of national competition authorities. Even if the Commission believes that a national authority's decision is wrong, it should not necessarily take over the case. National authorities may make mistakes, and national administrative courts are there to correct them. There must be some special reasons for the Commission to take over a case even when it thinks that a national authority is wrong. Also, as disagreements in antitrust cases are mostly about facts, the Commission, which has not itself heard all the evidence, should be slow to conclude that an authority is wrong. The Commission, after all, has only rarely intervened when national authorities adopted decisions under national law which were plainly quite different from the result under Community law, and even when national authorities approved, under national law, practices clearly contrary to Community competition law, contrary to the Ahmed Saeed principle.[12]

—It might be desirable to disclose to the parties before a national competition authority the fact that other authorities, or the Commission, disagree with the decision, if that is the case, (although the views of national authorities on Commission decisions as expressed in the Advisory Committee, are not disclosed). Knowing that there were official doubts might encourage an appeal. Companies would probably dislike the idea that the outcome of a national authority's procedure might be influenced by views, even non-binding ones, which they had not seen, even if their normal procedural rights entitled them to

---

11  This can be done at present under Art. 9 of Reg. 17. It is intended that there should be a similar provision in the new Regulations, but for use only in cases of disagreement.

12  1989 ECR 803.

comment on the substance of the points made before the decision was adopted. A company whose complaint is dealt with by one national authority might urge it to consult the Commission, or a national authority in another Member State, and would want to know whether it did so and what the result was.

—The Commission cannot be bound by a decision of a national competition authority, even one based on Community competition law. However, on the basis of the Commission's proposals, the only circumstances in which the Commission would take a decision in a case in which a national authority already had prohibited an agreement, would be (i) if new evidence or additional parties emerged, and the national authority had dealt with only part of the case or (ii) in the rare situation in which the Commission would give a favourable decision on the basis of undertakings (although it is hard to imagine such a case in which the national authority would first have prohibited the agreement).

## VII. Concerns expressed—courts

Most of the reactions to the White Paper have been broadly favourable, although almost all have pointed to specific issues which will need to be clarified in due course, or to specific problems which might arise. These do not seem to be objections to the principles proposed in the White Paper. However, several concerns have been expressed which, if they were valid and could not be dealt with, might amount to basic objections.

The first of these concerns is, that some people think that national courts are not well suited or able with confidence to apply Art. 85(3) (now 81(3)). I do not find this convincing, and before mentioning possible solutions I should say why. National courts have always had to apply Art. 86 (now 82). Art. 86 is frequently very much more difficult to apply than Art. 85(3). The problem that the parties are unable to obtain as much evidence as a competition authority could obtain if it investigated the case fully is likely to be more serious than the alleged difficulty for a court of deciding whether there is sufficient progress, or a sufficient share for consumers, under Art. 81(3). The problems of the inadequacy of the evidence available for production by the parties are at least a great, when defining the market or assessing, (in essential facilities cases) whether a claimant which is denied access could ultimately build its own facility, as the problem of deciding whether users are getting a fair share of the benefit, under Art. 85(3). If it is said that a 'fair share' is a policy issue or an ethical one, the answer is that courts have to decide similar issues in many cases, and though they may not find it easy, they are able to do it when necessary. If national competition authorities can do it, courts can do it. Like any other judicial function, it involves applying a principle to the facts of each individual case: it does *not* involve deciding how much benefit the courts 'want' consumers to get. There is an extensive decision-making practice of the Commission applying Art. 85(3), which has given rise to little (perhaps surprisingly little) controversy. Matra[13] is almost the only case

---

13 Case T-17/93, Matra Hachette 1994 ECR II 595. There have, of course, been many cases in which the parties challenged the refusal of an exemption under Art. 85(3).

in which the *grant* of an exemption under Art. 85(3) has been challenged (unsuccessfully). In practice the Commission accepts as sufficient consumer benefits such as the early introduction of a new product on the market, and accepts that if the market is competitive the benefits of cost savings will be adequately shared with consumers. This is hardly 'policy', and it is not sophisticated economics. Clearly courts could do it.

It is for the judges, the legislature, and the Ministry of Justice or the equivalent in each Member State to decide if this concern is justified, and if so to what extent. Insofar as, rightly or wrongly, some action to solve the difficulty is thought desirable, there are a variety of measures which could be taken. In any individual case, a court which considers it unsatisfactory to decide the issues between the parties on the basis of the evidence available to them (e.g. because it knows that its judgment will be regarded as a test case or because it wants to avoid any risk of conflict with a Commission decision) could adjourn to allow the market to be investigated by a competition authority,[14] or ask the authority to make submissions to it. In jurisdictions where judges were accustomed to do so (such as Scotland, where judges sometimes sit with financial advisors in company reconstruction cases), the courts might sit with economic advisors, if there were any suitable advisors available. Judges could, if they wished, have some training in antitrust economics. Specialised competition courts could be set up, formally or informally: the Kammergericht in Berlin, which heard appeals from the Bundeskartellamt until the latter moved to Bonn, was *de facto* a specialised competition law court. If the Commission could help the national court[15] with any information, it could be asked to do so. If the court found it useful, the national competition authority could be asked to make specific submissions on each of the four requirements of Art. 85(3), but such submissions would inevitably be cautious unless the authority had itself investigated the case, in which situation the court might be wise to adjourn until the authority had come to a formal decision. This would not, of course, be binding on the court, but it would clearly be helpful.

There is however, another, rather different, risk, which is that national courts might too readily accept that all four requirements of Art. 85(3) are fulfilled, merely because they were more accustomed to enforcing contracts than to applying competition law. This risk is avoided insofar as competition authorities deal with each case before the courts do. One solution to this problem is for commercial disputes

---

14 The Spanish Supreme Court has taken the view that courts should not decide Community competition law cases unless they have first been investigated by the national competition authority. This seems too strict, and indeed inconsistent with the direct effect of Community law and the duties of courts to apply it. But in some cases such a cautious approach might be wise. One important kind of case where a national court may feel the evidence before it is insufficient is where the parties have wholly unequal financial interests in the outcome: a small company with a modest claim may not produce enough witnesses to counter the large number of witnesses produced by a large company with strong reasons to argue that it is not dominant and that its constant practice with all its customers or suppliers is not an abuse.

15 See the Commission Notice on co-operation with national courts on the application of Arts. 85 and 86, OJ. No. C-39/6, 13 February 1993. This has been little used and is not likely to be extensively used: see Temple-Lang in vol. IV, XVIII Congress, Fédération Internationale pour le Droit Européen (Stockholm 1998).

involving competition issues, as well as appeals from competition authorities' decisions, to be dealt with by a specialised competition court. However, a better solution, which would help whichever court the issue arose in to decide it, is outlined below.

The third concern is a broader one. It is said that the effect of empowering national competition authorities and courts power to apply Art. 85(3) will be to increase the number of cases referred to the Court of Justice under Art. 177, and that this will add to the already excessive workload of the Court. The suggestion discussed immediately below is also intended to help to reduce the Court's workload.

## VIII. A 'Community Law Adviser' or 'National Advocate General' in each Member State?

One idea which would help to solve these problems has recently been discussed informally, and gathered support. Each Member State should have an independent Community Law Adviser, preferably a member of the judiciary, who would be available to advise national courts, at their request, on any issue of Community law (*not* only Community competition law) which was raised before them. The suggestion (which is not mentioned in the Commission's White Paper) was first developed for Central European States whose courts, when they join the European Union, will not be well prepared to apply Community law. The idea, which is a relatively simple one, is that each Member State should appoint a lawyer with enough experience and standing authoritatively to advise any national court which thought it useful on any issue of Community law—whether the issue should be taken seriously, whether the answer was clear or uncertain, whether a question should be sent to the Court of Justice, and if so how the question should be drafted. The aim is to give courts with little time to research Community law a well-informed and objective source of information and advice about it, so that they could decide how to deal with Community law questions quickly, correctly and with confidence. The opinions of the Adviser would not be binding on the court. In other words, there would be a standing *amicus curiae* or national Advocate-General on EC law issues in each Member State. Some national courts now ignore Community law issues because they feel they do not know enough about them, and this is unsatisfactory (and indeed contrary to their duties under the Treaty). The Community Law Adviser in each Member State could also provide advice to the national legal aid and advice service, and information to citizens, especially foreigners living in the State in question.

The main advantages of Community Law Advisers would be that the application of Community law by national courts would be facilitated, improved and strengthened, and that there would be fewer references to Luxembourg (because national courts would have an adequate, quicker and more convenient source of guidance which would be sufficient in most cases). References, when necessary, would be better focused. Community law would be more widely, more frequently and more uniformly applied. Appeals up through national court systems on EC law issues would be less common. The national courts themselves, with specialised advice, would be able to select only the more important or more difficult cases to send to Luxembourg. There would also be the important advantage that neither transfer of cases nor specialised courts would be needed: each court before which an issue of Community law arose would decide it (subject to an Art. 177 reference if really worthwhile). The Adviser, unlike the Court of Justice, would also be able to help the national court to *apply* the Community law rule to the facts of the case (often the real difficulty) if the national court so wished. Since the Court of Justice is advised by an advocate-general in all cases, national courts should not feel that it is a criticism of their knowledge to be advised by a kind of national advocate-general.

This idea could be adopted in any Member State without any Community measure, and without waiting for the others. It would be cheaper and more efficient than a major expansion of the European Courts. It would help to solve problems which may exist because judges find it difficult to apply any rules of Community law. It could therefore be used to help national courts to apply Community competition law, if any such help was thought useful: it would usefully complement the Commission's proposals on decentralisation. It would also provide the Commission (although the Advisor would be a national judicial post, *not* a Community one) with a useful source of information on legal problems emerging in each Member State, and if there was an Adviser in each Member State, differences between courts over Community law issues would be noticed before they led to problems.

One more aspect of this should be mentioned. At present all references under Art. 177 are to the Court of Justice, but the Court of First Instance hears appeals from the Commission in competition cases, and is more of a competition court than the Court of Justice. If the Treaty was amended to allow it, references under Art. 177 in competition cases might be more efficiently dealt with by the Court of First Instance than by the Court of Justice. Again, this idea raises wider issues.

## IX. Concerns expressed—legal certainty

A second concern which has been expressed is that if notifications are no longer possible (except under the Merger Regulation), the legal position of parties to restrictive agreements will be uncertain. It is of course correct that the (theoretical) right to insist on receiving a formal decision from the Commission under Reg. 17 would disappear. However, the vast majority of notifications are and have always been dealt with without a formal decision. Some lawyers already advise that notification is not worthwhile, in certain cases. Administrative letters, whatever their legal effects are exactly, give less legal certainty than formal decisions. Although Art. 86 is much harder to advise on than Art. 85, companies hardly ever notify under Art. 86, and they voluntarily choose whichever legal uncertainty results. The vast majority of restrictive agreements which are notified are signed and acted upon before the notification is made, so the parties are not waiting for Commission approval and are accepting any legal certainty that there may be.

There is now a large body of case-law of the Community Courts, and very many decisions of the Commission under Art. 85. More group exemptions and Notices are planned. When new problems arise, the Commission intends to adopt Notices and decisions as precedents. Companies with small market shares will anyway be exempt under the new group exemptions. Companies with large market shares can afford to pay lawyers and rely on their advice, as they already do under Art. 86. Large companies' joint ventures will come under the 1998 amendment to the Merger Regulation. In most other areas of law, notably tax law and patent law, companies rely on their lawyers and have no right to get prior official approval for what they are doing.

The Commission will, if its proposals are adopted, have power in difficult cases to adopt favourable decisions accepting undertakings from the parties to agreements and making the undertakings legally binding. In addition, a kind of equivalent of business review letters in US antitrust practice is being considered, which would say that the Commission saw no objection to the agreements described. The Commission would have no legal obligation to write such a letter in any individual case, and would write one only before the agreement was entered into (if the agreement is already made, the parties are not dependent on or waiting for Commission approval). Such a letter would bind the Commission, under the principle of legitimate expectations, but presumably would protect the parties against claims for compensation in national courts.

## X. Benefits and consequences of the system proposed

The most important benefits of the new system are reduced costs and delays for industry. There would be no unnecessary notifications, few multiple procedures, and no waiting for the Commission's reaction. Unnecessary differences between national laws will be reduced, and national authorities will more and more apply either Community law or national competition laws based on Community law. So companies will be able to use a single antitrust compliance programme, with only small modifications, for the whole Community.

The new system will mean substantially increased responsibility for lawyers and companies. Lawyers will have to advise whether draft agreements are valid and lawful, not merely whether they should be notified. Antitrust compliance programmes will be more important than they are now, since the validity of agreements may depend on whether there are additional restrictions of competition which would make group exemptions inapplicable.

Insofar as national notification procedures are retained, companies which want the maximum available legal certainty may notify to national authorities instead of the Commission. This may lead to national authorities having too many unnecessary notifications.

Because lawyers will have to take the responsibility for advising companies what they can and cannot do, there will be an even greater need than there is already to clarify lawyers' duties, under professional ethics, rules of not to mislead Community and national competition authorities, and not to help clients to break the law. This will require an effective response from European lawyers' organisations, which they have for years failed to provide on these issues.

This paper has already mentioned some procedural questions on which harmonisation of national rules will be called for. The present situation is that there is a considerable degree of convergence or harmonisation of substantive national competition law, but so far no harmonisation of the procedures of powers of national competition authorities, or of the penalties which can be imposed by them, and no harmonisation of the civil law consequences of infringements. In the long term, pressure for harmonisation in these areas can be expected.

# Chapter Three: Practical Implications of Reform

## NICHOLAS GREEN QC*

## I. Introduction

In the White Paper of the 28 April 1999 the European Commission has suggested certain ostensibly radical changes in particular to Council Regulation 17/62 EEC which, it is hoped, would, if adopted, lead to the decentralisation of European Community Competition law and a considerable increase in the flexibility and efficiency of the enforcement regime. It is the view of the Commission that, whilst Regulation 17 has worked well over the past 35 years, its time is ripe for radical amendment. Its principal vice is that it centralises power in an administrative body, namely the Commission, which manifestly is no longer able to devote sufficient resources to processing all of the myriad cases which come before it. It will hardly come as a surprise to practitioners to be told that delays within the Commission are integral and endemic. Moreover, these delays have become such a feature of life that they have been given judicial recognition by the ruling of the Court in *Automec* v. *Commission*[1] where it was held that, as a result of the dis-equilibrium between supply (administrative resources) and demand (notifications, complaints etc.), it was lawful for the Commission to prioritise its work in circumstances where adequate remedies existed elsewhere, for instance before the national courts.

It is difficult to quarrel with the proposition that the Commission is under-resourced relative to the number of cases pending before it. For this reason whilst the Commission's proposals may themselves give rise to numerous problems, when implemented, there may be little option but to undertake radical review and reform of the present system. The view of the Commission is that it must have a procedural framework which enables it to re-focus its activities on combating the most serious restrictions of competition whilst, simultaneously, permitting the decentralised application of the competition rules. Furthermore, such procedural reforms, as are adopted, should not be permitted to undermine the maintenance of consistency in the development and application of competition rules and policy throughout the Community and should also ease the administrative constraints on undertakings whilst securing legal certainty.

## II. The options

The Commission's proposed options focus on improving the authorisation system presently in place, and, switching to a directly applicable exemption system. The

* Brick Court Chambers, London.
1 Case T-24/90 (1992) ECR II-223.

*J. Rivas and M. Horspool (eds), Modernisation and Decentralisation of EC Competition Law, 31–38.*
© 2000 *Kluwer Law International.*

White Paper appears to suggest that these are mutually exclusive options. However, it may well be that changes to the Commission's internal procedures would be needed even if the Community went down the line of switching to a directly applicable exemption system. The Paper identifies four ways in which the existing authorisation system may be improved. These are:

(a) Changing the interpretation of Art. 81 so as to include analysis of the harmful and beneficial effects of an agreement in the assessment under Art. 81(1);
(b) Decentralising the application of Art. 81(3) to national competition authorities upon the basis of the centre of gravity of the case;
(c) Broadening the scope of application of Art. 4(2) of Regulation 17/62 EEC;
(d) Piecemeal simplification of procedures such as abolishing the requirement of translation into all Community languages and the simplification of the Advisory Committee consultation procedure.

### III. Rule of reason

One striking point arises from the first of these options. The Commission suggests a shift in the interpretation of Art. 81. The gist of the Commission's proposal is not however entirely clear.[2] Though, it appears to entail the Commission interpreting Art. 81 as incorporating a 'rule of reason'. The Commission observes that this would ease the notification constraints imposed on undertakings since they would not be required to notify agreements in order to obtain negative clearance. The Paper continues by stating that the Commission has already adopted this approach to a limited extent and has carried out an assessment of the "pro" and "anti" aspects of restrictive practices under Art. 81(1). A number of observations may be made about the suggestion. First, there appears to be confusion in the mind of the Commission between the facts and matters which are taken into account by Art. 81(3) and those which may already be taken into account, upon the basis of the consistent jurisprudence of the Court, under Art. 81(1). On almost every occasion when the Court has considered questions as to the scope and application of Art. 81 it has emphasised that Art. 81 does not operate in a vacuum and all of the surrounding economic circumstances must be taken into consideration. For many years the Court has emphasised that Art. 81 *is* subject to a rule of reason. It is thus something of a surprise to read that the Commission has been using the rule of reason sparingly in its own analysis of cases to date. One would have thought that the rule of reason was such a well-established principle of Community law that it would have been the norm, not the exception, within the Commission. At the risk of over-simplification the rule of reason entails the regulator (be it Commission, National Authority or Court) examining the overall objective of the agreement, arrangement or practice in issue and deciding whether it is pro-competitive or, at the very least, neutral of competition. If the overall analysis of the agreement leads to the conclusion that it is

---

2 See White Paper paras 56 and 57.

pro-competitive or neutral of competition then the secondary question arises: what are the essential contractual building blocks necessary to achieve that pro-competitive or competition-neutral end result? The logic being that those essential clauses must, by definition be acceptable if in aggregate they do not exert any anti-competitive effect upon the market. The carrying out of such analysis does not, in my view, necessarily permit the decision maker to take into consideration all of those facts and matters which would otherwise be inserted into the equation under Art. 81(3). There is hence a dichotomy between Art. 81(1) and (3). The former is concerned with the narrow question whether an agreement impacts materially upon competition. If, upon analysis, it does then the secondary question arises whether there are other benefits (not related to competition) which are of sufficient magnitude to offset or counter-balance the proven restrictive effects of the agreement. For illustration, if an agreement has an appreciable yet not excessive impact upon competition the fact that it may improve production techniques or lay the groundwork for further innovation and may increase employment may constitute 'macro'-economic considerations which justify, as a matter of policy, the anti-competitive effects of the agreement which necessarily are attendant upon it. The point to be made is that the rule of reason does not, upon the basis of present case law, necessitate the decision maker in taking into consideration the criteria which necessarily will be assessed under Art. 81(3).

In summary on this point there are two conclusions to be drawn. First, the Commission should already be applying, as a matter of course, the rule of reason to each and every agreement which comes before it. Secondly, without a re-writing of the Treaty it is difficult to see that there is any competence for the Commission or other decision maker to take account of Art. 81(3) type considerations in determining whether an agreement or practice materially restricts, distorts or prevents competition. Moreover, the rule of reason is an approach which national courts and competition authorities should, in any event, adopt in the name of good case management. To judge by the practical experience of competition cases before the English courts, where Judges have grasped the doctrine of the rule of reason with enthusiasm, it provides the Courts with a robust means of disposing of cases quickly, including at an interlocutory stage, upon the basis that viewed in the round a clause which is, ostensibly, a fetter on individual commercial freedoms, is incapable on any sensible view of restricting, distorting or preventing competition. The Courts have had considerable experience of such an approach in the context of the doctrine of restraint of trade and something of the approach which the courts have traditionally adopted in the context of that doctrine has rubbed off in their approach to the rule of reason.

## IV. Procedural simplification

With regard to the other three suggestions mooted for improving the authorisation system there is less to be said. The Commission has expressed some scepticism about its proposal regarding the notion of allocating exemption competence based upon the 'centre of gravity' ('Schwerpunkttheorie') of a case. The criteria for determining the centre of gravity of a case would be not only the effects of the agreement or practice in question but also the need to safeguard competition effectively. However, as the Commission observed, this option does not reduce the total number of notifications but merely distributes the total number of current and future cases between the Commission and the national competition authorities. Moreover, it does not make it possible to increase action against the most serious infringements which are almost never notified. Its effectiveness is further limited by the fact that notifications which are liable to be handled by the national competition authorities are few in number. Additionally the decisions of the national authority are enforceable only within their own territory and thus cases involving several countries can neither be handled in this way nor according to the centre of gravity theory. Further, the Commission is concerned that the proposed criterion for allocating cases is insufficiently precise to permit notifications to be allocated along clear-cut lines. The Commission recognises the centre of gravity concept is well suited to the allocation of complaints as between competition authorities but would be difficult to apply in allocating notifications. In short, the Commission does not believe that this would be the answer to its present woes. So far as the broadening of the scope of application of Art. 4(2), which waives the prior notification requirement for a number of different types of agreement, the Commission observes that an advantage of such a change for the undertakings concerned would at least be that even in the event of a late notification the Commission would be empowered to assess whether the restrictive practices were worthy of exemption and could be exempted retroactively. Undertaking legal certainty would be enhanced by such a means. Nonetheless, the Commission returned to its central complaint, namely that such a modification would not limit the Commission's scope for re-focussing its activity on the most serious restrictions of competition since it would maintain its monopoly on granting exemption. Finally, the Commission's suggestion for piecemeal procedural simplification is said to have major disadvantages in that it could exert, not a de-centralising effect, but a centralising effect, enhancing the incentive for undertakings to notify their restrictive practices to the Commission. The Commission's criticism appears to be that the present degree of procedural inefficiency under which the Commission's procedures belabour operates to deter notifications; whereas, an improvement in the efficiency of the Commission would encourage notification. Given the Commission's present concern to encourage de-centralisation this, otherwise, perverse logic appears to be correct.

## V. The de-centralisation of exemptions

The principal theme underlying the White Paper is that the Commission's monopoly over the right to grant exemptions should be abolished and that the right should be exercisable by both the national competition authorities and the national courts. It is to this issue that I now turn. There is little doubt that the de-centralisation of the power to grant exemptions would substantially lessen the work load of the Commission. If that is the overriding objective of the Commission then the proposal will be a resounding success. However, so keen is the Commission to present this proposal as the panacea to all ills that, with respect, it overlooks some of the problems which such de-centralisation will necessarily, and in my view, inevitably, entail. That is not to say that the disadvantages which will accompany de-centralisation necessarily undermine the Commissions central thesis. Only that the excessively rosy picture painted in the White Paper requires toning down before a proper perspective can be obtained on the Commission's central proposal.

Put broadly, the Commission advertise and promote their de-centralisation theme by reference to a number of perceived advantages for legal certainty and for undertakings. In particular there is the ever present suggestion that de-centralisation will accelerate the processing of cases, will reduce the scope for delaying tactics, and will reduce the cost of enforcement to undertakings. All of these things are said to enhance legal certainty.

Starting with the suggestion that de-centralisation will accelerate the processing of cases it has to be questioned why this should necessarily be so. The assumption that speed of processing will increase assumes that national competition authorities have the resources and experience to process notifications more rapidly than the Commission presently does. An increased work load for the national authorities is inherently likely to slow down the decision making processes within the authorities themselves barring a large increase in national administrative resources. National competition authorities will have to apply national competition law in parallel with Community competition law and the fact that their case load will increase surely suggests that the speed of processing will decelerate. So far as the courts are concerned they, at present, have jurisdiction to apply only Art. 81(1). Certainly within the United Kingdom this has encouraged the courts to adopt, as observed above, a robust approach to the proper analysis of Art. 81(1) since this has enabled them to dispose of cases relatively quickly and economically. However, if Art. 81(3) becomes part of the armoury of a defendant facing an allegation that a particular agreement infringes the competition rules then the task confronting the national court will be considerably more complex. Certainly, the amount of evidence which will need to be adduced by both Claimant and Defendant to assert and rebut advantages of the sort contemplated by Art. 81(3) will be very substantial. Although not an exact parallel the recent decision of the Restrictive Practices Court in *Director General of Fair Trading* v. *Premier League, BSkyB, BBC* (July 1999) suggests that full pros and cons analyses of agreements can be lengthy and expensive affairs. That is not to say that every time a party raises Art. 81(3) by way of defence the case will assume the proportions of Premier League litigation. However, it seems to me correct that the litigation will expand substantially in time and cost. As such, even if Judges continue to pursue a robust approach to the rule of reason this will not necessarily result in the more rapid resolution of cases. Conceivably, Judges will take an even more robust approach to the rule of reason if the alternative, of finding an arguable case of restriction, is to condemn the Defendant to a protracted trial on the pros and cons of its agreement. The conclusion reached is that de-centralisation of the power to grant exemptions will not necessarily expedite the processing of cases either before the courts or before the national competition authorities.

Turning to the relationship between the various enforcement bodies concerned, at present, in those Member States where the national competition authorities are not permitted to apply the EC Competition rules, there is a triangular relationship between the national courts, the Commission and the Courts in Luxembourg. In those Member States where the national competition authorities *are* permitted to apply European competition law, the relationship becomes quadrangular. In the White Paper the Commission expressed criticism of those cases, before national courts, where the court has stayed the proceedings to permit the parties to pursue a notification before the Commission. The Commission has made clear that it will not necessarily give priority to those cases which are stayed before national courts if they do not, otherwise, possess intrinsic importance. It is certainly true, at least judging by the experience of the English courts, that when there are dual proceedings before the Commission and the national court, the national courts will generally give way to the Commission ordering a stay of proceedings pending a determination by the Commission upon the notification or complaint. Indeed, the Courts have even gone so far as to stay proceedings to permit one or other of the parties to then effect a notification upon the basis that the Commission is better suited to the adjudication of a particular issue than the national court, particularly in the light of its exclusive jurisdiction under Art. 85(3).[3] There is no reason to believe that strategic applications for a stay of proceedings would be any the less likely if there is a de-centralisation exemption power to national courts and authorities. A party confronted with a claim that its agreement is illegal under Art. 81(1) is always in a position, forthwith, to effect a notification to the national competition authorities and then argue before the court that the national competition authority is a more experienced and better forum for the determination of the exemption formula than the court. Judges are likely to be sympathetic to such an approach given their relative lack of experience in competition law matters and such enthusiasm may be heightened by the desire to remove from an already over-crowded court list a case which would otherwise absorb a considerable amount of court time. There is, accordingly, no reason to believe that there will be greater access to the courts and a greater willingness on the part of the courts to engage in complex anti-trust litigation simply because the courts have a greater power to exempt an agreement which is, *prima facie*, caught within Art. 81(1).

Finally, the de-centralisation of exemption formula is, for the reasons given above, unlikely to reduce the cost of litigation. On the contrary, the obligation of the national courts to examine what may, in practice, be an enormous array of competing benefits and dis-benefits is likely to increase, not reduce, costs.

The philosophy of the Commission, as set out in para 99 of the White Paper, appears excessively optimistic. The Commission state simply that national courts are close to European citizens and since the inception of the Treaty they have had a specific role in safeguarding the rights of individuals within their jurisdiction which are conferred directly by Community law. Whilst this is undoubtedly true, it does not even begin to meet the obvious procedural difficulties which will arise under a system of de-centralised exemptions.

## VI. Consistency

Another concern of the Commission is to maintain the consistent and uniform application of the competition rules if there is de-centralisation. This is sound policy.

---

3  See, for example, *Williams and Cardiff RFC* v. *Welsh Rugby Union and Others* (1999) EuLR 195.

However, one of the points made by the Commission[4] seems to me to be plainly misguided. The Commission point out that de-centralised application of the competition rules must not be allowed to stand in the way of the maintenance of the conditions of competition that are consistent throughout the Community. This is a preface to the Commission asserting its primacy over all other enforcement agencies and identifying areas where, in the case of conflicting views between the national competition authorities and courts, on the one hand, and the Commission, on the other hand, the Commission should be able to intervene in order to 'put matters straight'. The Commission recognise that national courts or authorities may take a different view of the facts than the Commission. In such circumstances it appears to be the Commission's implicit belief that the national court or authority will inevitably be wrong and it, the Commission, will inevitably be correct. Thus, in para 102(2) the Commission states:

> When a national authority has adopted a positive decision which is either no longer open to appeal or which has been confirmed on appeal, or a court has delivered a positive judgment ... which is either no longer open to appeal or has been confirmed on appeal, *the Commission can always intervene to prohibit the agreement, subject only to the principle of res judicata that applies to the dispute between the parties themselves, which has been decided once and for all by the national court.*

With respect to the Commission this appears to be an instance of intellectual and bureaucratic arrogance. It assumes that the national competition authorities and courts which, as the Commission emphasises elsewhere, are often much closer to the real facts than the Commission, must always bow down to the superior wisdom of the Commission. This appears to ignore that the duty of co-operation imposed upon the institutions of the Community by Art. 10 (formerly Art. 5 EC) apply in one direction alone. However, this is not correct. The duty of co-operation applies as much in the relations of the Commission towards national competition authorities and courts as it does in the relation of the latter to the former. In circumstances where the national competition authorities and courts have undertaken an exhaustive analysis of a problem and have concluded that it does not exist, it would appear disproportionate for the Commission to trespass upon that decision. Indeed, it is often the case that a more exhaustive analysis may be undertaken at the national level than at the Community level. Certainly, in truly adversarial proceedings before courts information may emerge which simply never sees the light of day before the Commission. If there is to be true de-centralisation of competition law to the national competition authorities and courts the Commission will have to exercise a strict self-denying ordinance in order to uphold confidence in such de-centralisation.

## VII. Conclusion

In conclusion, the Commissions thesis that de-centralisation is necessary may represent sound policy. However, this should not blind one to the obvious difficulties

---

4 See para 102(2), p. 35.

which will necessarily follow from implementation of this policy. The existence of such difficulties may not, in themselves, be a reason not to pursue the policy but they should not be under estimated as they appear so to be in the White Paper. This paper addresses only a very small number of the implications of the White Paper, from the perspective of a litigator, but even from this perspective it is apparent that if reform is to be undertaken great care will be needed in devising the detail.

# Chapter Four: The Anti-trust Epidemic—Causes and Prospects

BILL BISHOP*

When Mark Attew asked me to participate in this conference, I told him that it might be interesting to give a talk which put Competition Law into perspective. The arrival of competition law in so many member states is part of a much wider phenomenon all over the industrial world and no one has studied to any great extent the process by which competition law administration develops over time. I want to put forward a life cycle hypothesis of competition law. I suggest that there are basically three phases that can be found in the administration of any competition law; from the first legislation enacted in about 1890 right up to that being enacted today.

The first of these three stages is Phase 1—the phase of barmy enthusiasm—which is usually relatively brief. Then comes Phase 2—slick superficiality—and finally Phase 3—earnest economics. The Americans have certainly reached Phase 3. We here in Europe are generally speaking towards the end of Phase 2 and beginning to move into Phase 3. The Commission's notice on the definition of the relevant markets, being so clearly economic in character, was the most important single event in the transition from Phase 2 to Phase 3.

Turning first to Phase 1 to substantiate the claim that there is indeed a period of barmy enthusiasm at the beginning, I will consider just three countries, starting with the United States which was more or less the first to develop competi-tion law (although Canada has a prior claim). In an 1895 case—the US against Knight—the US supreme court said 'the Sherman act does not apply to a sugar cartel because the act is concerned with commerce and commodities come before commerce in the economic process' (this particular cartel being concerned only with commodities). This is no doubt very sensible logic if you have forgotten to turn on your brain.

Next is an example from Canada. The Canadian law enacted merger control legislation shortly before 1960 and this quote is from that year—a court decision in the BC Sugar case in which the only two sugar refineries of Western Canada merged. The transaction was challenged before the court which ruled 'it is not an offence against the act for one corporation to acquire the business of another merely because it wishes to extinguish a competitor'. It would take the wisdom of Solomon to decide whether the Canadian court in BC Sugar or the American court in *US* v. *Knight* was the more idiotic.

My third example features a relatively recent arrival to the competition law business—the Czech republic. The Radegast Brewery merger in 1997/98 was actually a

* Lexecon Ltd., London.

J. Rivas and M. Horspool (eds), *Modernisation and Decentralisation of EC Competition Law*, 39–47.
© 2000 *Kluwer Law International*.

case in which I had some peripheral involvement so I must confess that my views of the episode might be affected. The Competition Authority ruled that the merger would enable the merged companies to become so much more efficient than their competitors that they would be able to lower prices to consumers—thus driving small breweries out of business. For this reason the merger was deemed to be anti-competitive. *In defence of the Czech authority it has to be said that this idea of greater efficiency as a detriment to the merger, something that Fred Genie has called the efficiency offence, is hardly unknown elsewhere.* The essential nonsense of such a view was vigorously pointed out to the competition authority and a few months later exactly the same merger was *approved* on exactly the grounds on which it had been turned down six months earlier.

## I. The world wide epidemic

I started by saying that we were going through an epidemic of new competition legislation. About 30–35 countries have adopted competition law during the 1990's. A grand total of approximately 80 countries around the world now have competition laws of some description; many of whom are really very tiny. Professor McNutt said earlier that he worried whether Ireland may not have been in some respects too small a unit within which to administer competition law. But Ireland is a behemoth compared to some of the other countries with their own competition legislation. When Richard Whish and I were in Malta last summer at a meeting of the Islands and Small States Association concerned with competition law, we found that people from all over the world were there—from the Caribbean and the Pacific, from little mountain fastness' to even littler sub-states. Jersey, with a population of 100,000, has recently adopted a competition law, as have the Faeroe Islands with a population of perhaps 40,000. Just consider, the Faeroes are an archipelago, 100 km or so long with the population spread out along the archipelago and no town larger than 15,000 inhabitants, and yet they have an equivalent of the Office of Fair Trading. The mind boggles! Indeed, Malta itself has a population of only 300,000 making it smaller than a good number of *cities* in the UK.

The question of why this phenomenon has occurred is an interesting one. I consider four basic reasons to explain why countries adopt competition law.

(1) Fashion
(2) Rent-seeking
(3) Headline chasing
(4) Economic efficiency

I consider numbers (2) and (4) to be the ones of real interest, but it is worth giving some consideration to number (1)—fashion. There has certainly been an element of following fashion in the adoption of competition law around the world. It seems that having an anti-trust law nowadays is similar to the desire for a national flag or a national airline in the newly independent states of the 50's and 60's. You were not quite the real thing unless you had that particular accoutrement.

The second reason is rent-seeking—especially by lawyers and consultants. Whether competition law does much good for anyone is an open question, but there is no question that it does benefit the legal services industry, and it has to be admitted, the odd economist too.

To explain the idea of rent-seeking a little further. What it really describes is people seeking to get a guaranteed profit for themselves without much further work. Economists call this a rent. The idea has emerged from the economics of public choice; a new area of economics which developed after the second world war. It has since become a major research field; indeed James McCannon—one of its founders—was given the Nobel prize in economics about 15 years ago for effectively inventing the field. The idea of public choice economics is to take the methods of economics and apply them not in the normal commercial sphere but in the public sphere. The traditional approach held that governments and voters operate in the *public interest* whereas analysis of markets assumed that *private interest* was the motivation. This seems an almost absurd dichotomy and in truth the public interest theory of government is almost universally recognised as a complete failure. No-one could possibly explain the activities of most modern governments by reference to a public interest theory. It is much better to make the same assumptions across all sections of life and allow that people are pursuing the same self interest in the ballot box as they are when they visit the supermarket to spend their pounds. Public choice economics sees political parties as being similar to firms in an oligopoly offering products called policies with customers spending their votes to buy these things. It is then possible to model what bureaucracies and legislatures, for example, do and don't do. The supply and demand for votes and for policies lies at the root of such models.

In this way, the public choice approach connects to another fundamental idea of economics—that a substantial amount of monopoly is created by government. Some scholars at the University of Chicago about 20 years ago used to argue quite vigorously that not only some but *all* monopoly is a result of governments. This is perhaps taking it too far, but it is certainly clear that a great bulk of monopoly power is an emanation of the state. I will expand on this later.

The third explanation for the proliferation of competition law is headline chasing by politicians and consumer pressure groups. This is not completely distinguishable from the 'fashion' motivation. Headline chasing certainly plays a part in the adoption of laws. I am old enough to remember the rash of countries in the 1960s who adopted ombudsmen legislation. This vestigial nonsense of ombudsmen persists all over the world; it is clearly an idea whose time has passed but still survives in the world of ideas because of the fashion that swept through the news media in the 1960s for anything Scandinavian.

The fourth theory is that competition law promotes economic efficiency. This is the principal theory, whose truth is simply assumed by most people when they write memos to governments on what a good thing it would be to have a competition law. In fact there is very little evidence that economic efficiency either generates competition law or is the effect of competition law. Everyone who has ever studied this question has concluded that the efficiency effects of competition law are at best puny compared to deregulation, low taxation and a culture friendly to entrepreneurship. If you plot on one axis an index of anti-trust rigour and on the other index annual GDP change you will see no visible relationship between the two and nor has anyone ever been able to detect one.

Let me now consider the question of the constituents of a good anti-trust system from a public interest point of view. In my opinion, there would be four main features. First, effective deterrents of cartels; second, effective removal of barriers to entrepreneurship; third, sophisticated merger review and fourth, avoidance of waste and harm on all other topics. The fourth element may seem an odd constituent to emphasise, even obvious, but in fact one of the worst features of competition law is that it may become a charter for rent-seekers of every kind. In particular, people whose aim has nothing whatsoever to do with competition but is actually the intervention by the authorities to the detriment of someone else's business. How well have anti-trust laws since 1890 corresponded to this ideal? In my opinion, and this is very much a matter of opinion, that answer is that anti-trust practice (at least in the second half of the 20th century for which I can claim some familiarity), has been an almost complete failure.

The sources of this failure are fourfold; firstly it is often complainant-led; secondly it may be resource constrained; thirdly, it is economically naïve; and fourthly displays no concept of a cost-effective use of resources. To consider the first failure; to allow antitrust policy to be complainant-led is one of the worst decisions a competition authority can make. Competitive complainants should normally be turned away; instead, officials think that the mere fact that someone is complaining is evidence for wrongdoing and must be treated seriously. Competitors complaining is usually a sign that there is something *right*, not something wrong. An extreme example of complainant-led failure occurred in the UK where the OFT spent two or three years and gave rise to public and private expenditure well in excess of £30 million on what was essentially a commercial dispute between two branches of the television industry. It was effectively a situation in which the cable companies tried to get the whole industry regulated in ways favourable to themselves rather than their principle rival—direct to home digital satellite. The conclusion of this process was the complete failure of the OFT's case before the restrictive practices court.

The second type of failure is resource constraint. Most competition authorities have been far too resource constrained; they really do not have the resources to do a sophisticated job. The principal exception has been the US, mainly because it is funded by an ear-marked tax and so resources are abundant. The truth, of course, is that it is not called an earmark tax but a filing fee under merger notification. However, given the large number of mergers in the whole US economy and given that the filing fee is $45,000 regardless of size, the total revenue amounts to a couple of hundred million dollars. In other words, the US agencies do, in effect, have a tax on transactions which funds their activities—and you more or less get what you pay for in competition law! It is not accidental that the sophistication of the US enforcement procedure is clearly and significantly superior to that of every other country.

The third item in the anatomy of failure is economic naivety. Markets and economic life are generally complex. It is not possible to develop simple little rules for not very bright bureaucrats to apply, or even not very bright judges for that matter. There is no substitute for careful consideration of possible theories combined with careful empirical testing and analysis to decide which theory is correct. It is only recently that this has been recognised in Europe. The Americans have been practising this for a little longer, although by no means very long. Even the roots of this in the US go back no further than the issuance of the DoJ guidelines in February 1982.

The fourth source of failure has been the lack of a cost-effective use of resources or more especially, a lack of any real concept of it. Just consider the complete insanity of the system which existed in Brussels for 35 years in which the principal activity of enforcement officials was to read through notified contracts to find some piffling little item for which some far fetched theory might lead you to think a different contract term would lead to more competitive markets. Of course, sitting down at your desk, taking out the in tray, managing the back-log and doing nothing in particular is frequently alarmingly attractive to bureaucracies. We are again in the area of public choice; what is it the bureaucrats really want to do? Fortunately, the European Commission—with its discussion of vertical anti-trust—is on the point of jettisoning this waste of resources.

Turning to the question of the key problems facing the new European national authorities, I think that there are four main points to consider. Firstly, national focus is natural; secondly, information is scarce; thirdly, serious market analysis needs resources; and fourthly the effect of the 'Mandarin model'.

The first, then, is that the focus of these authorities is inevitably national. But that will almost inevitably introduce bias into the process and lead to some wrong decisions. To give an example; in 1993 the Commission correctly ruled that Pilkington competes in a market at least as wide as northern Europe. Although the Commission decided that the relevant geographic market was wider than the UK it would take a strong competition authority faced with a complaint against Pilkington—which supplies more than half the glass in the UK—to rule that they were not dominant because they faced competition from Saint Gobain in France and various other players in other countries. And yet that would be the right decision. This problem is related to the second problem—that external information is scarce. The salient point here is that national competition authorities have no power to demand information outside the boundaries of that member state. It is in fact quite difficult for them to acquire such information; the writ simply does not extend that far. Yet such information is necessary, not only for determining geographical markets but also for benefiting from the sorts of natural experiments which happen when different situations occur in other countries.

The third problem is that serious market analysis needs resources. I have already mentioned the US' *de facto* 'ear-marked tax' which, although no one formally classifies it as such, is exactly what it is.

The fourth problem may be called the 'drag of the Mandarin model'. The Mandarin model is one of the curses of European government. The European ideal of administration is to establish a permanent bureaucracy members of which remain for the duration of their career. These institutions recruit people in their early 20's by examination and then leave them in position for 40 years. This is an appalling way to run enforcement; just compare European Competition enforcement (whether in Brussels or in the member states) with that in the US. In the US leading academics enter and leave the bureaucracy, as do highly talented lawyers from private practice. This enriches the bureaucracy, and also enriches academic life in both economics and law when these people return to academia. It enriches private practice as well, in that a great many people can be found to advise companies who have a real knowledge of how anti-trust enforcement operates. Various poor excuses are advanced against this view; they tend to highlight the issue of the revolving door and such like. But in practice the Americans solve these problems of bureaucracy, and no objective observer could deny that the quality and consistency of American enforcement far exceed that of any other system in the world. The person who should head the bureaucracy or its major divisions should be the best person who can be found anywhere to do the job; and the selection should not be limited to people who were judged to have passed an exam some 25 years ago.

I need not spend too much time on the proposition that economics now lies at the heart of this business. John Temple-Lang said as much this morning. The SNNIP test for market definition is overtly economic in character and has a history of adoption around the world. It was first announced and adopted in the United States DoJ Guidelines in 1982. It was adopted by the EC officially in 1997 in the notice on market definition but in fact appeared earlier in the 1992 Nestlé/Perrier case. The test was adopted by Canada in 1991, New Zealand in 1996, Australia in 1995 for telecoms and, as I understand, more generally since then. Other countries have not officially adopted it but it appears semi-officially. The UK sponsored a research paper in 1992. Since then the UK guidelines under the new Competition Act effectively conform to the SNNIP test. Italy also sponsored a paper, written there by an insider rather than an outsider in 1995. Even the monopoly commission in Germany claims that German law conforms to the economic ideal; a claim treated with incredulity by those familiar with the actual behaviour of the Bundeskartellamt.

## 1. Economic advice and resources

It is certainly true, as John Temple-Lang noted earlier, that there is an uneven availability of economic advice and resources across Europe. There is a division between the UK on the one hand, and the rest of the Community on the other. There is an active competition culture here in London, with a number of competing firms of economists who offer advice to governments and especially to private companies. There are many *academic theorists* in the rest of the Community, but applied anti-trust economic skills are scarce and firms of competition law economists virtually non-existent. Europe's competition industry is effectively centred on London, although, in my opinion, London does not serve the non-English speaking member states particularly well. Economics companies work best with teams of people discussing cases, and there are simply very few occasions when a sufficiently large group of speakers of other European languages can be found within these firms to form effective units.

## II. Rent-seeking

I said earlier that government is the source of most monopoly; let me expand on this point. All of the following are instances of governments creating control over prices; patents, tariffs, land use control, anti-dumping duties, licensing, government contracts and government regulation. Some of these might be good and defensible, but there is no denying that they restrict competition. There is no doubt that there is a demand for regulation; interest groups will use any available means to get the coercive power of the state to protect them from their competitors. Some of you may be familiar with the Messerlin thesis propounded by Professor Patrick Messerlin of the Institut des Sciences Politiques in Paris. Messerlin looked at the pattern of anti-dumping duties and of anti-cartel enforcement in Europe, and discovered a very interesting pattern. He suggested that the best predictor of anti-cartel activity by DG Competition was the anti-dumping activity of DG Trade two years previously. This result actually makes perfect sense; DG Trade has been the poodle of interest groups ever since it was set up. Even the crassest anti-consumer claims get a sympathetic hearing in that particular bureaucracy. One of the exasperating features of economic life is that disagreeable foreigners such as Japanese and Koreans frequently compete against you, so if you want to have a nice cosy European cartel, and essential first step is to keep these "damn foreigners" out. So the process of cartel formation consisted of first, going along and knocking on Dr. Baisler's door in DG Trade and saying 'please Dr. Baisler, please make it expensive for the foreigners to serve European consumers' Of course, it was not put quite like that, but that was the effect. Then of course, when Dr. Baisler had obliged which he seemed always to do, the European producers could heave a great sigh of relief and book the hotel in Switzerland where they could meet in agreeable circumstances to set up the price fixing and market sharing agreement. You may think that this sounds a bit pat, but Patrick Messerlin found that the pattern is actually there—you can go and look at it.

All this leads to an important conclusion; that the administration of competition law is in effect a decision about intervention and the informal regulation of the economy. If care is not taken, the 'enforcement' of competition provisions can become a web of regulation acting in favour of one interest group and against another. This phenomenon is fairly widespread around the world. The clearest example from the UK is the BSkyB saga; in which BSkyB effectively began to be regulated under competition law in the first year in which it became profitable. The competition authority saw it as an extraordinary transition from insolvency to monopoly in a space of less than 18 months. Between 1995 and 1998 BSkyB had imposed upon it accounting separation, detailed rules of reporting and a detailed rate card, all of which was in effect negotiated with and partly specified by the competition authorities who were acting in response to elaborate representation from the cable companies. This was all supposedly under the banner of preventing an abusive dominant position. A man from Mars looking at it would say it was just another regulated industry—and it is.

What, then, are the antidotes to rent-seeking? Above all an enforcer needs a compass—and that compass must be the interest of consumers. They must ask; Is there market power that harms consumers? Are there barriers to entry that are artificial and ought not to be there? If so, intervene—otherwise do not.

To illustrate the importance of this, I will mention just three types of application of Art. 82, (formerly 86), all of which have an equivalent in the legislative copies which have replicated virus-like in the member states. The first is the prohibition of predatory pricing. In effect, this can turn into price regulation—an imposition of a price floor—and into market share allocation. There is one instance of this that, if I ever wrote a memoir of my years as a consulting economist, I would deal with on the first page. I was advising a big company who had a small competitor. This small firm approached the larger one seeking a market sharing cartel and was rebuffed. Then a few months later the big firm got a letter from John Temple-Lang no less, saying that the Commission was somewhat disturbed by a complaint it had received from, of course, the erstwhile small company. In fact the big company had no intention of poaching the small company's customers, but it decided that it would make an emollient response to the European Commission. Enforcement of a prohibition on predatory pricing under Art. 82 was, for the small company, a pretty effective substitute for cartelisation—which was its real aim.

The second application of Art. 82 is the doctrine of access to essential facilities. Once again it involves John Temple-Lang who invented this doctrine that in the first of the Ports cases (Spring 1993 I believe). The relevance of this doctrine is that it is not just a shield against being cut-off, but can also be a crowbar by which to open up vertically integrated industries so that complainants can demand supply at whatever point in the supply chain they would like to be supplied. I hope that the *Bronner* case will put some brakes on this process, but the implications in terms of the possible regulation of vast numbers of industries are truly alarming.

The third idea to consider is the goal of promoting competition. This aim is surprisingly widespread; I have seen it in Sweden and the UK in the last year and I am sure this virus has spread much further. Anyone who considers OFTEL, the UK telecoms regulator, will see it in extreme form. OFTEL is not shy about saying that it regards a fall in BT's market share as a measure of its success. They seem blissfully unaware that bureaucratic management of industries of this sort is extremely undesirable and contrary to principle. This is what happens, however, when a bureaucracy becomes dedicated to a theory that is in fact simply an excuse for favouring one pressure group over another.

## 1. What is to be done?

I have a modest proposal. I would make governments—including executive agencies, local authorities, the governments of Scotland and Wales etc.—subject to competition law. There would be fines for any attempts to use government powers for anti-competitive purposes. Companies which try to procure anti-competitive actions by councils or governments could be also fined. In addition I would have a legal ban on subsidising campaigns to stop planning permission for competitors. The cost to industry of the problems I have described is not trivial. Consider the increase in costs over the last 26 years since the UK's succession. In 1973, I know for a fact that there were only about 20 people in the whole of the UK who would have classed competition law as their speciality. At that time, the costs to UK industry were pretty tiny—I would estimate £3 million or so per year. Today there are about 800 lawyers who earn their living as competition specialists. The total cost to industry amounts to at least £350 million a year form this source alone, and it is growing. I conjecture that by the year 2010 there will be perhaps 1500 competition lawyers and the cost to industry will be £600 million or so (in today's money)—but it could be double that.

## 2. What should an authority do?

I have a simple programme. First, vigorous cartel detection as has been recommended by scholars beginning with Bozner and Borke in the 1970s. What was then iconoclasm is now orthodoxy. Second identify uncompetitive sectors within the economy. It should be easy to set up research programmes in order to learn from the different practices of nearby similar countries—and yet this is rare. The important sectors of the economy should be identified and then resources concentrated on these areas. Third, competitor complainants—personally I would have no truck with them. Competitor complainants should be left to seek remedies before the courts. This would require them to face the costs of complaining and seeking regulation in their favour. It would not be funded by the tax payer or divert resources from pro-consumer activities. Fourth, a good competition authority should make a contribution to public debate and public education in a democratic society. It should call attention to state created monopoly. This is not the sort of thing which will earn you a knighthood being often inconvenient for governments—but it might actually do something like make a difference to prosperity and economic life.

## III. Final assessment

### 1. What are we to say about competition law 1890–1999?

The history of competition law, unfortunately is largely an account of failure; of ineffectiveness and service to rent-seekers. But there is some hope in the anti-cartel movement now sweeping the competition authorities of the world; once again the Americans are leading the way. But it is not clear how important this will be and, more to the point, it does not remedy the other problems I have highlighted. In this sense the future of competition law remains doubtful. Competition law is here to stay, but the only thing that we can be sure of is that it will enrich the legal services industry. Whether it will do any good is wholly a matter for conjecture.

# Chapter Five: The Appraisal of Vertical Agreements: Competitiveness, Efficiency, Competitive Harm and Dynamic Conduct

PATRICK McNUTT[1]

## I. Introductory remarks

The publication of the Commission's *White Paper* on modernisation of the rules implementing competition has generated considerable debate. It proposes a radical review of the existing enforcement system. For the past two years[2] the Commission has been modernising its competition policy (a) to ensure it reflects contemporary economic realities and, in particular (b) to prepare it for the challenges of economic and monetary union and Community enlargement. The *White Paper* should also be seen as an important complement to the project on vertical restraints, which led to the new block exemption Regulation (adopted by the Council in June this year). Other speakers have addressed legal issues arising from the proposals contained in the *White Paper*. This paper paints a picture on a rather large canvass in which issues relating to European competitiveness, to the block exemption and to the need for consistent[3] economic assessment, will all compete for your attention.

Consistent economic assessment is recognised by the Commission as an important goal. The principles underlying European competition policy (as applied to vertical restraints) have been anchored to an economics based approach. The primary objective of the wide ranging and flexible block exemption is to grant companies which lack market power (and most do), a safe harbour within which it is no longer necessary for them to self-assess the validity of their agreements. The Commission (and national authorities[4]) will now make use of market share caps to link the exemption to market power. Economic assessment that is consistent, clear

---

1 Professor Patrick McNutt is Chairperson of the Competition Authority in Dublin and Research Associate, University of Dublin. The views expressed here are strictly personal and do not reflect the views of the Authority or the University of Dublin. The usual disclaimer applies.

2 *Vide* 1997 Competition Report paras 36–50, 1998 Competition Report paras 24–35.

3 Consistency would have two tests: (a) consistency across Member States in the interpretation of the rules of competition to avoid forum shopping and (b) consistency with respect to the standard: harm to competition v. harm to competitors. There may be a tendency, where competition authorities have responsibility for both competition and consumer protection, for a case to have the characteristic of both competition and consumer violations but once the evidence is garnered the economic emphasis may change or the legal theory may change between competition and consumer protection law during the course of an investigation.

4 For example, the Irish Authority's *Category Certificate and Licence* (in respect of agreements for resale) Decision no. 528, December 1998, included a 20% and a 40% market share threshold.

*J. Rivas and M. Horspool (eds), Modernisation and Decentralisation of EC Competition Law*, 49–68.
© 2000 *Kluwer Law International*.

and comprehensive enough to provide clear guidelines for compliance on the basis of legal advice and sufficiently flexible to accommodate the emerging corporate actions and strategies in the new Europe, will have a crucial role to play in a system of concurrent jurisdiction (paras 14 and 15) wherein the Commission, national authorities and national courts apply their respective economic assessment skills.

In marked contrast to US antitrust law, where the effective decisions are taken by the courts, the current EU system[5] gives the Commission, an administrative body, the exclusive right to confer exemptions. The influence which the Commission is able to exert upon the content and form of agreements affecting trade between Member States, through this exclusive right, has been greatly increased by the passing of block exemptions. However, nobody disagrees that the Commission has made its competition law an instrument of market integration. But national authorities may have different goals and take different approaches to interpreting Art. 81 (previously 85) and 82 (previously 86). It is also possible that exemption decisions by national authorities may be appealed (to the High Court in Ireland), and the national court may subsequently refer the matter to the European Court of Justice.

The judiciary may have to improve upon their respective economic skills as a direct consequence of decentralisation. The increasing volume of EU competition case law (so characteristic of US antitrust law) may help. While the author shares Professor Korah's view[6] that the proposals contained in the *White Paper* would bring more work for economists as the case work will depend more heavily on economic reasoning, the author has argued elsewhere[7] that national judges should hear (independent) economic arguments from a source other than from the parties to a case and their expert witnesses. This is particularly important today where different and challenging competition concepts are being applied and where the detection of tacit collusion ('concerted practices' of Art. 81) is the main problem facing competition authorities.

For whatever reasons, the apparent failure to utilise[8] Art. 13 to take over some investigative tasks from the Commission does not augur well for the proposals (paras 82–98) contained in the *White Paper*. It may have had more to do with a resources constraint than any lack of goodwill across Member States. Sadly, that lack of resources remains a problem and may continue to be a problem, thus frustrating the enforcement efforts of national authorities. However,[9] the number of conventional antitrust cases notified to the Commission have stabilised, which is an encouraging development in support of the *White Paper* and probably due in no uncertain terms

---

5 On the other hand, the key issues of EU competition policy are really points of law and hence the CFI does exercise the ultimate influence.

6 Speech delivered to IBC's EC Competition Law conference in London, May 1999.

7 Views expressed in a paper by McNutt (1999): entitled 'Market Definition, Dominance, Abuse of Dominance' prepared for FTC Jamaica conference, Mimeo 1999.

8 While we are all familiar with the Advisory Committee set up under Art. 10 of Regulation 17 to discuss draft decisions, we should recall that Art. 13 of Regulation 17 envisaged Community and national authorities working closely together whereby the Commission would delegate to national authorities some of its enquiries which were essentially national rather than Community-wide in scope.

9 *Vide European Community Competition Policy* Report 1998, paras 4–6.

to the new *de minimis* Notice. Likewise, the increase in the number of merger notifications is probably correlated with the drive towards European competitiveness,[10] as European undertakings merge in preparation for the single European (economic) market.

## II. European competitiveness

### 1. Compliance and competitiveness

The move from *ex ante* to *ex post* decentralised enforcement will usher in a new era where the Commission, national authorities and national courts co-administer the competition rules. Co-administration insofar as one understands the proposals (para 107) will allow the Commission to intercede in any judicial review of an Art. 81(3) court ruling in a Member State and/or to remove a case from the jurisdiction of a national authority. Since the decision of a national court can be registered throughout the EU under the Brussels Convention, parties to a transnational business agreement may opt to forum shop as the decisions of any two national authorities or courts need not be the same. This will give rise to inconsistent decisions and a risk of divergent policy that would frustrate the Commission's objective (para 15) of ensuring consistent application of the rules. One observer[11] has remarked that as a goal, European competitiveness requires consistency, clarity and legal certainty, commenting that

> this very uncertainty is likely to distort commercial projects which will be crafted to fall under the Merger Regulations ... [the] Merger Task Force will be flooded with notifications.

Consolidating the single market[12] is of prime importance in ensuring that economic and monetary union is a success. Boarman[13] in the context of a debate on US antitrust, re-echoed a theme that is of particular relevance to our discussion here today on modernisation and decentralisation:

> The proponents of relaxation questioned the premise of antitrust, namely, whether it, in fact enhances internal competition. There was a particular concern that the anti-merger provisions of the Clayton Act has the inherent potential of reducing economic efficiency. And that there was anxiety that the Sherman Act

---

10 *Vide* Special Issue of *European Business Review* entitled: 'A Political Economy Perspetive on European Integration', vol. 96, no. 5, 1996.
11 Stephen Walzer senior counsel at BAT, writing in *Global Competition Review* edition, August/ September 1999, p. 13.
12 *Vide* para 63, p. 25, *European Community Competition Policy*, 1998.
13 At a microeconomic firm-specific level management engage in strategic rival behaviour while at a more macroeconomic level a closer look at the direction of EU competition policy *viz.* competitiveness is required. *Vide* Boarman (1993) 'Antitrust Laws in a Global Market' *Challenge,* January and Bangemann (1993) 'Industrial Policy and International Competitiveness' in *EC Frontier Free Europe.*

prohibited to US firms, *certain collective actions designed to achieve international objectives* that were readily available to foreign firms [my italics].

It has often been commented[14] that companies (within Europe) contemplating business arrangements, particularly vertical agreements, react strategically[15] and are prepared to gamble with the competition regime.[16] We have to acknowledge that modern European firms not only require a competitive and efficient distribution system but also a competition regime that keeps legal uncertainty to a minimum. Indeed the Commission has to remain keenly aware of the contribution of European competition policy to achieving that level of international competitiveness (consistent with achieving a single European market).

## 2. The meaning of competition

The link[17] between competitiveness and competition has been identified in EU policy:

> The primary objective of the European Community's industrial policy is to increase *international competitiveness* of European firms. To achieve this ... build on the economic strengths which undoubtedly exist in the Community ... these include demanding standards and a skilled workforce. Even more important, however, is a business environment geared towards competition so that there can be *fair competition* between European firms [my italics].

It has been recognised by the Commission[18] that the ongoing business integration and restructuring process 'adds an extra dimension to the analysis of vertical restraints', offering a 'springboard for competitiveness' in increasingly global and competitive world markets. One could infer from such comments that the international competitiveness of European firms as envisaged by the Commission as early as 1990, more poignantly now in 1999, is intricately linked to a business environment which has the hallmarks of *fair competition* interpreted in the strictest sense of competitiveness and fair trade. However, the European business environment is unquestionably imperfectly competitive[19] characterised by rapid product development, new

---

14 *Vide Financial Times article* 'Protecting Exclusivity', 1 October 1996.

15 In other words, if a rival firm introduces an agreement with a supplier in a product-market, a follower–leader strategy is adopted by competitor firms. While this response is a type of cooperation, it is a competitive response.

16 The *White Paper* proposes to remove the notification system—thus placing a greater ones on companies and their legal advisers to self-assess their agreements or actions for compliance with competition rules.

17 As early as 1990s—in this speech delivered by Bangemann the emphasis on competitiveness is noted.

18 *Vide* Chapter II, para 70 of the *Green Paper on Vertical Restraints*, 1997.

19 The environment could be characterised by Schumpeter's cycle. This cycle of 'creative destruction' continues whereby innovation creates dominance which gains monopoly profits which stimulates new innovation and new dominance and cocooned within that evolution of market structure, typical of the 1990s firm development, is the presence of vertical restraints.

product technology, market alliances, market sharing strategies[20] and vertical arrangements.

Such characteristics are (arguably) reminiscent of Clark's *workable competition* in so far as product differentiation, excess capacity and rewards for innovation (Schumpeterian efficiency) have all been used to show the *absence* rather than the presence of competition. While barriers to entry, independence of action, price leadership and number of competing firms have all been judicially embraced, product differentiation, excess capacity and rewards for innovation have not. If product differentiation, excess capacity and rewards for innovation (all directly contrary to perfect competition) are desirable, perfect competition as a standard is clearly not, workable competition clearly is a standard. Competition authorities will have to re-evalute their approach to firm conduct[21] and may have to recognise that firms can compete on dimensions other than price—such as innovation, product variety and product quality. That debate is elsewhere;[22] suffice to mention here that characteristics of the WWW-Internet markets, in particular, low entry barriers, no national borders and zero[23] marginal costs, may become the hallmarks of a new competition dynamic in the new system envisaged by the *White Paper*.

## 3. Voluntary notification and adverse selection

The Commission acknowledges (para 77) that voluntary notification has failed to detect serious breaches of the competition rules. Not surprising—with voluntary notification there is an adverse selection process at work. Wils[24] (1999), however, captures the essence of voluntary notification:

> The notification and exemption system as set up in Regulation 17 acknowledges the problem of certain types of easily concealable violations being unlikely to be notified under any prescreening system in that it *does not provide for a legal obligation to notify all agreements* but only creates incentives to notify by granting notified agreements immunity from fines and by making agreements falling

---

20 Vertical arrangements are increasingly recognised by business as the supply-chain (mode of entry) into product-markets, designed specifically to enhance both the efficiency of distribution while maintaining effective competition in markets. The new competitive markets in which modern firms are operating in the latter part of this century are fundamentally different to the 1960s on two important counts *viz.* the strategic nature of rival management behaviour (which impinges on inter-brand competition) and the structural changes in distribution (for example, a move towards greater centralisation of distribution) arising in Member States as they move to a more open and competitive single integrated European market.

21 More importantly by interpreting conduct in a dynamic context.

22 For example, non-price competition has emerged as a competitive aspect on the Internet as price competition is so cut-throat. Buyers can surf to other digital dealers sites to check prices and suppliers can do the same. With such competition on price, suppliers find themselves competing on customer service and delivery and on the design and presentation of the e-commerce sites.

23 Interesting to note that if marginal cost is constant, mergers will always increase price. Modern firms, however, are faced with negatively sloped demand curves and decreasing industry costs.

24 Wouter Wils (1999): 'Notification, Clearance & Exemption in EC Competition Law: An Economic Analysis', *European Law Review*, vol. 24, no. 4, April.

under Article 85(1) which have not been notified, unenforceable even if they fulfil the conditions of Article 85(3) ... [A]s the problem of the excessive number of notifications and the resulting impossibility for the Commission to deal with them swiftly, *no time limit* has been provided for the Commission decision—the undertakings *are free to implement the notified agreement* and when the Commission later adopts an exemption decision, *this decision can have retroactive effect* back to date of notification. In the interim, the undertakings *benefit from immunity from fines* [my italics].

The hallmarks of voluntary notification are in *italics*—they are conducive to an adverse selection problem. While the Commission may have to take cognisance of the concerns of some Member States about the need for prior control of horizontal agreements, companies, under the umbrella and impetus of European integration, should be encouraged to self-assess. For those actions which are certain or likely to constitute violations but for which *ex post* enforcement does not work, for instance, because the probability of detection is low or the threatened sanction is insufficiently high, the party will have no reason to notify. The solution is for *ex post* enforcement to work.

## 4. Effective enforcement

*Ex post* enforcement is at the heart of the Commission's *White Paper*, where the argument is made throughout the paper, that resources and enforcement are positively correlated. There are at present, and probably will continue to be, big differences between national authorities in 'size, professional expertise, experience and effectiveness'. Effective enforcement[25] of Community competition law depends on effective decentralisation:

> If a national authority were consistently lax or protectionist, or so legally inefficient that its actions are frequently annulled by national courts, or had been 'captured' by the companies ... or if it was not subject to effective judicial review or if it was simply too small to do its job fully ...

the opportunity cost of time and resources devoted to notifications is high. If *ex ante* actions are likely to be detected and sanctioned as violations *ex post*, parties will have no incentive not to notify. However, there may be a chance that they will get cleared *ex ante* either just by accident or because the national competition authority has insufficient information *ex ante* to assess the action correctly. Wils has suggested

> a more important measure [is] to deprive the prescreening decision, at least the clearance decision, of its final character, leaving open some possibility of ex post

---

25 John Temple-Lang (1997) 'Community Antitrust Law & National Regulatory Procedures' in Fordham's *International Antitrust Law & Policy*.

prosecution or litigation. In the most extreme case, the status of the decision could be reduced to that of a private legal opinion, which either precludes any later prosecution or litigation nor has any authoritative value.

Such a presceening system has some merit; it amounts to public provision of legal advice. With the arrival of new Member States this may still serve a function in situations where knowledge of competition law by the parties in the Member States is limited or where private legal advice is not satisfactorily available.

## 5. The goal of European integration

Coincidentally, the arrival of new Member States introduces a bigger picture[26]—the wider political implications of the *White Paper* in a new Europe witnessing the development of a political European state where public (utilities) monopolies are being supplanted by private (utility) oligopolies and where restructuring is creating an oligopoly structure across European businesses. This political momentum will have an important bearing on how national authorities inevitably function under the proposed new proposals. The Commission at a macroeconomic[27] level will have to continue to give guidance on the issue of large size. Competition policy is well grounded in principles[28] that questions large size[29] and while national authorities may differ on economic methodology, there will be little room for difference once decentralisation requires national decisions to have community-wide effect. In other words, a convergence on the application of economic principles will be required, particularly if the Commission is proposing that national authorities and courts run the 81(1) and 81(3) assessment together and not separately.

The goal of European integration is paramount: Europeanisation of competition policy necessarily elevates the goal of *economic efficiency* in appraising competition cases. The Commission[30] did allude to efficiency wherein it recognised that traditional distribution channels were in decline. The Commission also recognised (without an explicit endorsement) that—although well advanced amongst US industries—*cooperation* between product manufacturers and retailers in the supply

---

26  From a competition policy perspective, this would probably have implications for the definition of geographic markets.

27  Macroeconomic in the sense of extending borders; a review on the position of trade marks in *Silhouette* judgement, for example, would allow international exhaustion.

28  One could argue that the genesis of US competition policy is anti-firm and that the genesis of EU competition policy, Arts. 85, 86 within the Rome Treaty 1957, is European integration (pro-consumer).

29  Although size in invariably measured by market share, where authorities impose market share thresholds below which conduct is deemed anticompetitive. But size of firm and size of country widely differ across Member States—10% of the UK market for product *X* does not easily compare in measuring market power with 10% of the Irish market for the same product.

30  *Vide* Chapter 1, paras 40–43 of the *Green Paper on Vertical Restraints*, 1997.

chain is still in its infancy in the EU. In the *White Paper* the Commission opines (para 50):

> one of the objectives in modernising the competition rules must therefore be to *avoid impeding cooperation* between undertakings, where such cooperation does not pose any threat to competition [my italics].

Therefore compliance may be intricately linked to a non-intrusive competition policy—one that proffers legal certainty rather than proscription of corporate activities *per se*. In other words, the point must be made that hostility to efficiency and co-operation runs counter to the goals of political union and to national economic goals—more efficient firms contribute more to economic growth.

## III. Vertical agreements

### 1. Lessons from vertical agreements

One reason why we allude in this paper to vertical agreements is precisely because the *White Paper* should be seen as complementary to the block exemption. The debate on vertical agreements provided a range of economic issues[31] germane to the debate on modernisation and decentralisation. In fact, if the *White Paper* proposals enter into force *circa* 2003, the significance of the vertical restraints reform will be reduced somewhat. Arguably, once the Commission has agreed on what precisely constitutes international competitiveness, it will have to examine the likely ramifications for the application of competition policy in Member States. If it involves an acceptance of large size (an economies of scale argument), national governments may interpret this as heralding national champions. And will Member States be precluded from using competition policy to protect its own interests against the behaviour of foreign-based firms? If the main protection against domestic monopoly power is imports, then the effectiveness of competition policy depends on the protectionism of trade policy. In other words[32] trade policy becomes more effective the greater the number of foreign firms in an economy. However, as competition policy makers, we must not forget that foreign competition is not a perfect substitute for domestic competition.

### 2. An Achilles' Heel

It would help enormously if there was economic analysis or reasoning attached to the *White Paper*. For example, one could at least infer from the economic reasoning

---

31 For example, the concept of a market and separate markets, market share thresholds, supply chain and IT advances and the overlap with horizontal effects and international competitiveness.
32 *Vide* the discussion in McNutt (1994) *Perspectives on Competition Policy* CIEL University of Ulster.

contained in the Commission's draft *Green Paper*, a view that competition and cooperation, however defined, however intangible, were not antithetical. A view to the contrary emanates from a traditional *static* view of the world of market structures, a view that was not appropriate in the context of supporting the economics underpinning vertical restraints and a view that is wholly inappropriate in the current debate on modernisation. Corporate restructuring (for example, the adoption of vertical arrangements and/or mergers) reflects the more *dynamic* nature of modern business behaviour. Intuitively what is happening in the world of business is a move towards obtaining cost leadership status in the industry. And consolidation helps to deliver that goal.

The bottom line for competition authorities at the coal face of integration, is that cross-border consolidation[33] is inevitable; indeed one may argue that it should be encouraged by government (and by competition authorities) through the removal of legal, fiscal, regulatory and political barriers to entry. This would allow the emergence of efficient competitors. The *Realpolitik*, against which the *White Paper* is set, is one that favours the emergence of European competitors rather than national champions. And it has to be recognised that the main players will be the national competition authorities. There is in my view a need to continue to re-examine[34] the economic criteria applied to (horizontal) agreements, so that national competition authorities can agree on the 'right' market definition and on the appropriate welfare measures (discounted for innovation) to be used in assessment.

The economics of the new single integrating Europe will require competition policy to be wedded to a detailed consideration of corporate strategies and to a broad coverage of firm interactions along a number of different dimensions. The economic standard therefore may have to be harm to competition not harm to competitors. Such a standard will ensure that European competition policy will remain focused, particularly in checking that national authorities do not derail the necessary integration process. Albeit, there are national markets, there are substantial differences[35] between national laws and there are substantial differences in procedures. With national markets,[36] different conclusions about effect may arise and different views on a necessary remedy may be needed in different countries. Derailment will not happen if there is European-wide consensus on the economic principles (and measurements) underpinning a Community-wide standard of harm

---

33 *Vide CEPR Bulletin*, no. 74, Summer 1999, and the discussion on European banking consolidation and competition concerns, quote 'if consolidation of the banking industries within individual European countries is undesirable for reasons of competition, it my prove popular nevertheless for other reasons'.

34 This would help anchor the removal of prior control of horizontal agreements to a well grounded set of economic principles that reflect the *real economique* of the new single integrating Europe.

35 For example, the range of mergers subject to control, whether that control is applied before or after the event, in addition to whether or not there is a notification system. The latter may no longer be the case anyway.

36 In the UK, for example, although competition is generally the only criterion, the actual legal test is of the effect on the public interest. Both these issues have led to detailed investigations in recent years. One part of the test under European law is of compatibility with the common market—not obviously relevant outside Europe.

to competition. The failure to achieve such a consensus may in the long term represent the *White Paper*'s Achilles' Heel.

## 3. The inevitability of 'large size'

As modern firms, particularly European firms, adjust to the challenge of achieving cost competitiveness, greater legal certainty[37] in the increasingly complex area of both horizontal and vertical arrangements and their impact on competition and efficiency is required. Business arrangements should be considered in the context of the grand EU design to achieve international competitiveness objectives. Vertical arrangements deliver cost efficiencies and offer modern firms the possibility to improve customer services, to penetrate new markets with existing products, try entry into new products thereby strategically defending an existing market share. We are inclined to adopt the position that a big firm gains some market power from its size *per se* but the effect of size may be small, especially if barriers are only a minor element of structure. Vertical arrangements can be interpreted as a partial substitute for vertical integration with probable efficient and pro-competition elements attached.

The theoretical argument on size, stems from a debate in the 1950s between Adelman and Bain[38] where Adelman had argued that size *per se* was entirely irrelevant to market power. Bain disagreed; introduced the height of entry barriers argument which infiltrated the economics of antitrust. Rather than rehearse the arguments, the position adopted in this paper is simply that a big firm gains some market power from its size *per se* but the effect of size may be small, especially if barriers are only a minor element of structure.

The significance of market power and entry barriers arises when market power is high as presented by the Commission[39]

> vertical restraints can also hinder the process. It must be stressed that such a negative outcome is likely only when *market power is high* and there are *barriers to entry*—in competitive markets vertical restraints are unlikely to hinder integration [our italics].

Large size comes into play significantly in merger analysis which presents a different yet related dimension on size—the use of market shares to infer market power. However, market shares do not provide a reliable signal[40] on market power of merging entities. The lack of confidence that the Commission and national competition authorities have displayed regarding alternative measures of market power may be associated with an over indulgence in the market share–market power axis. This will have to change in the new enforcement system.

---

37 Legal scholars may indeed argue that a block exemption regulation or a Notice issued by the Commission could eliminate much of the uncertainty which affects the majority of distribution agreements.

38 Adelman's chapter in G. Stigler (1955) *Business Concentration and Price Policy* Princeton and Bain (1956) *Barriers to New Competition* Harvard.

39 *Vide* draft 'Green Paper on Vertical Restraints' in chapter II, para 8.

40 I have been advocating the use of the $q$-ratio which enables us to measure profitability. Poor profitability, for example, can lead to a mix of exit and of merger activity in an industry.

It is important to recall that the Commission will retain prior authorisation on mergers (production joint ventures) under the new Art. 2(4) in Merger Regulation. Art. 2(4) applies to all joint ventures constituting a concentration within the meaning of Art. 3, albeit only

> to the extent that (they have as their) object or effect the coordination of the competitive behaviour of undertakings that remain independent.

From the Commissions' first case, an examination of Art. 2(4) effects has already displayed some common themes as reported:[41]

> The relative size of the Art. 2(4) market and the joint venture's market, which is assessed for dominance purposes, has been important in assessing the likelihood of coordination. Normally, the commercial incentives, and hence the risk of coordination, are smaller if the joint venture's market is significantly smaller than the Article 2(4) market.

However this cannot be considered sufficient condition for the absence of coordination between the parent companies. Such analysis is welcomed; it reflects a seismic shift away from the traditional[42] and reliable economics to embrace the new[43] economics. This shift in emphasis and approach is paramount in order to handle a new range of challenging economic issues—monopsony power, entry lags, supply substitutability, separate markets becoming joined, strategic interaction and tacit collusion. The EU Merger Regulation provides for a pure system of *ex ante* enforcement through prescreening. In the US, the Hart-Scott-Rodino Act 1976 similarly provides for premerger notification to the Justice's antitrust division. It would appear to be generally accepted that *ex ante* enforcement through prescreening is indeed appropriate for merger control. The fact that mergers are difficult to undo is not as such a sufficient reason to opt for *ex ante* control. It is precisely because the expected rents from anticompetitive mergers exceed the expected cost of litigation that any threatened sanctions would have to be very substantial. And also the competition culture in Europe is to threaten imprisonment for price fixing rather than involvement with anticompetitive mergers, so *ex post* deterrence is not really an option.[44]

---

41 *Vide European Community Competition Policy* 1998 Report, pp. 60–61.

42 New methods of quantifying monopoly abuse of dominance, for example, *q*-ratio, entropy, Lerner index and Harberger deadweight loss will have to be considered, *vide* McNutt (1999): 'Real Gains from Competition', Mimeo, 1999.

43 For example, transaction cost economics, law and economics and public choice approaches in addition to game theoretic advances in theory and game theoretic perspectives on competition policy.

44 As argued elsewhere, for notifications, *ex ante* enforcement through prescreening is unsuitable for Art. 81 because of the excessive administrative cost it entails, the number of contracts and business decisions to be controlled being enormous; for those agreements or decisions which are notified, the national authority is likely to have difficulties obtaining *ex ante* all relevant information about their legality, whereas certain categories of violations which are easily concealed, such as horizontal price fixing agreements, are unlikely to be notified at all.

## 4. Co-responsibilities

With three players, the Commission, the national courts and the national authorities multi-level principal-agent problems[45] will emerge, creating an additional degree of bureaucratic x-inefficiency (in theory) while raising the spectre of shifting the burden of decision making to under-resourced national authorities. Practical issues to do with the interplay between the Commission and national courts, the Commission and national authorities and between the courts and the national authorities and indeed between sector-specific regulators and national authorities (not withstanding Commission Notices) will have to be ironed out. While national authorities may be prepared to accept the new jurisdiction, one has to ask will Government secure adequate funding to allow authorities to accept the new responsibilities and management control functions. One is putting a marker down for governments to ensure additional resources in order to avoid x-inefficiencies occurring. And if a court wishes to draw on the expertise of its national competition authority to assist in the Art. 81(3) evaluation, then this will be a matter for national legislators to solve.

Any risk-averse national authority would then have to carefully consider any dilution of the Commission's exclusive jurisdiction of Art. 81(3) and weigh up the advantages in ensuring uniform interpretation and coherent application of the rules of competition. Reading this paper here in London, brings to mind one important aspect of the new proposals. National authorities back in Dublin considering a case under the Treaty rules will have to have the power, for example, to pass the files to authorities in London. And this will require a plan of future cooperation between competition authorities in different Member States, a plan that overcomes the *Spanish Banks* Art. 20 prohibition (para 96).

It could be inferred from the *White Paper* that the Commission is not relying on full cooperation as it allows itself the right to interfere by retaining the right to have the final say on any case initiated by the national authority. The involvement or interference would arise where the case was perceived to have a particular significance in a wider EU context or where the Commission perceived a threat to the uniform application of EU competition rules. *Apropos* my earlier point on competition v. competitiveness, would the Commission interfere with a national case when a large EU brand leader or its subsidiaries are parties to the agreement under assessment? Will competition principles be sacrificed on the altar of European integration?

In answering that type of question, one would have to elicit from the Commission the objective of European integration and further, to elicit from DG Competition, the role of competition policy towards achieving that objective. With regard to the objective of European integration, procedures for the application of Art. 81 should be developed following an economic interpretation of 81(1), to pursue simultaneously, the objective of safeguarding competition and that of European integration and to avoid the prohibition not only of dynamic behaviour which does not restrict

---

45 Typically monitoring costs. The Commission acting as principal with national authorities as agents describes the current *ex-ante* regime, which will be changed with the *White Paper* proposals.

competition but also of behaviour which promotes integration. The latter requires intervention only in cases where a business possesses significant[46] market power.

### 5. Interpreting conduct in a dynamic context

The Court of Justice has repeatedly held that the restrictive nature of non-price vertical agreements (for example, an exclusive distribution agreement) within the meaning of 81(1) can be considered only by reference to its *economic and legal* context. One aspect of the economic context, is in interpreting conduct in a dynamic context. The time needed to obtain an individual exemption is by no means as insignificant for the efficient operation of the markets, and particularly in today's business world. We have to recognise that innovation and supply-side entry are not only representative of modern corporate behaviour but are also the defining characteristics of the new economics of antitrust.

There is an obligation therefore on the Commission to establish coherent principles of competition around which companies can plan their strategies. For example, we can argue that it is only in the presence of firms possessing market power individually or collectively[47] that vertical (exclusive distribution) agreements can have an economic impact which restricts competition and thereby increases the undertakings discretionary monopoly power. Alternatively, we can argue that agreements can also restrict competition if they are conducive to horizontal collusion between producers and distributors. If an agreement or action does not have harmful effects on competition, then, arguably, no reason exists for introducing artificial obstacles to a firm's free choice of (optimal) organisational form.

### IV. Consistent economic principles

### 1. Consider alternative measures

Apart from Commission guidance, national authorities may have to consider what constitutes a competitive market when one deviates from the traditional perfect competition model. The answer is rather unclear. And less clear again is what constitutes an *efficient* competitive market. The Commission does not rule[48] out the possibility that potential advantages flowing from synergies may create or strengthen a dominant position. The neo-Chicagoan view, that integration cannot transfer monopoly power from one level to another, nor create more market power than exists from horizontal conditions, challenges the traditional view, that integration,

---

46 Decided cases show that the Commission places great emphasis on market shares and once these can be shown 'to reach 45% it becomes almost impossible to claim that such an undertaking lack-spower, unless there is another undertaking in the same market with a share of equivalent size (Goyder, *EC Competition Law*, 1990, p. 302)'. The explanation on offer in the Commission's *Interconnection Directive* 97/33/EC is that an organisation shall be presumed to have significant market power when it has a market share of more than 25%.

47 Therefore an examination of the market share is a necessary, but not sufficient, condition in this case.

48 *Vide* Commission decision AT&T/NCR.

by displacing open transactions, often forecloses the market and thereby excludes rivals. Vertical agreements[49] deliver cost efficiencies. In addition, we have to acknowledge that there are other equally important elements of structure[50] more relevant to an assessment of firm conduct in the 1990s.

As noted earlier, cooperation and competition are not necessarily antithetical. Today's insights derived from the theory of games, underpin a new approach to the detection of tacit collusion. It can help us understand that collusive outcomes are possible without there being anticompetitive behaviour. Crucially, we may have to modify or even abandon the more traditional and well tested measures of market power—the HHI and concentration ratios—and adopt new measures such as the $q$-ratio, the Lerner index and Harberger deadweight losses.

In its judgement 2 July 1992 on the Danish fur market, the CFI pointed out that

> in order to assess an exclusive agreement in the light of 85(1) of the Treaty, it is appropriate to consider the actual *economic context* in which it may have its effects [my italics].

In the same judgement it declared that

> depending on the facts and actual circumstances in which the market in question operates, an exclusive supply agreement may, by guaranteeing the producer sales of its products and the distributor security of supply, be such as to intensify competition in terms of the prices and services offered to consumers in the markets in question, thereby helping to improve the *interplay of supply and demand* on that market [my italics].

Here we see a struggle in understanding the dynamics of a market but using a static methodology. Alternatively, falling short of embracing a game theoretic approach, a dynamic analysis might suggest that the exclusive sales agreement was the more efficient mode of (supply) entry into the market in question.

## 2. Joint dominance and an irrelevance condition

The Commission has linked market share and market power. The author would subscribe to the view that dominance is not about market shares *per se*, it is about an ability to behave to a large extent *independently* of the firms' competitors and customers and independently of the consumer. This returns to my earlier point

---

49 Integration as a business strategy can be interpreted as a matter of degrees depending on the supply-chain network/economies of scale; compare integration in any two product markets, e.g. steel andread production and you will arrive at different conclusions. Rather than present a strict yes–no analysis we must recognise the redefinition of existing markets and the emergence of new markets with IT and internet advances. Vertical agreements are a strategic response to acquire economies of scale and scope. In other words provided the $x$-level of relative market share had no significant foreclosure effect, and that net economies are positive and welfare enhancing, the presumption of non-applicability of Art. 81(1) should apply to vertical agreements.

50 McNutt (1998): 'Legal Barriers to Entry & Compensation' in McGee [Ed.], *Commentaries on Law and Economics*. Dumont Institute for Public Policy Reseach/Legal Scholarship Network.

that we should rely on business to comply; they are the best arbiters of independent behaviour. National competition law should then assume that actions are rebuttable against a set of behavioural conditions.

The Court of Justice described a dominant position[51] as:

> a position of economic strength enjoyed by an undertaking which enables it to hinder the maintenance of effective competition on the relevant market by allowing it to behave to an appreciable extent *independently* of its competitors and customers and ultimately of consumers [my italics].

A common definition of dominance takes its authority from *Hoffman-La Roche* and emphasises the position of economic strength and how it enables the undertaking to hinder the maintenance of effective competition on the relevant market. Market share is obviously important in measuring strength but other factors,[52] for example, the entropy[53] in market shares, the extent to which the allegedly dominant firm has 'that freedom of action which is the special feature of a dominant position', low barriers to entry and the absolute and relative market shares, are equally important. One standard reference text,[54] Bellamy and Child (1993), implicitly accepts this when they argue that

> except in the most obvious of cases [ ... ] the proof of a significant share is seldom a substitute for a *full economic analysis* of the issues of dominance [my italics].

A full economic analysis must take account of business cycles and trends in corporate strategies. In early periods of US antitrust, economists struggled with monopolies, then oligopolies as the business cycle progressed. The interesting issue now for European competition policy as the *White Paper* appears are issues to do with joint dominance, collective dominance and oligopolies: what is the difference in pure competition law principles between all three? And is there any difference between Art. 82 and merger control? Against a European business background of changing corporate strategies, innovation and advances in IT and technology, the potential harmful effects of agreements need to be carefully and judiciously monitored and assessed by national authorities and the Commission. A full economic analysis should be mandatory. In other words, it is precisely because of changing corporate strategies and advances in IT and technology that potentially harmful effects arise and that it is incumbent on national authorities to identify the rents accruing and seek remedies that dissipate the rents. But we have to be able, if at all possible, to distinguish between tacit collusion and strategic interdependence amongst firms.

European competition policy is slow to embrace new economic approaches. What is beginning to happen, however, is the arrival of new legal concepts which

---

51  Judgement in case 85/76 *Hoffmann-La Roche* v. *Commission* (1979) ECR 461, paras 38–39.
52  The author alluded to the use of the $q$-ratio, for example, *vide* pp. 125–127, *Journal of Statistical & Social Inquiry Society of Ireland*, vol. XXVII, part IV. The $q$-ratio is a ratio of market asset value/reproduction costs: in a competitive equilibrium with zero monopoly rents, $q = 1$.
53  Entropy measures look at *redistribution* of market shares amongst firms.
54  Bellamy and Child (1993): *Common Market Law of Competition*, Sweet & Maxwell.

serve only to obfuscate the economic context of the analysis. There is a view that 'joint dominance' is a legal concept with no direct equivalent in economics. Broadly speaking, joint dominance is about coordination, yet there is no agreed test for joint dominance. In the Commission's view there are a host of factors in a market typically thought to facilitate coordination. The author would agree with Bishop[55] (1999) that what should not happen is that the analysis of joint dominance (or any economic concept) should be reduced to a 'box ticking' exercise with each market assessed on the basis of whether the products are homogenous, demand stagnant, the rate of technological change low, and so on. He argues that a major contribution of the *Gencor/Lonrho* judgement[56] is its explicit identification of joint dominance with the economic concept of tacit collusion.

In other words, if we interpret joint dominance as collusion in the economic sense, what is important in merger control is preventing coordination in circumstances where it looks likely that it could be sustained (in economic terms, where coordination is incentive compatible). In practice this means that is not enough to make a case that after the merger the remaining firms have an incentive to coordinate on a higher price. It must also be the case, that in the circumstances of the market, a sustainable mechanism exists by which the threat of lower prices in future will make it rational for them to stick to the higher price, despite the fact that in the short term they have an incentive to undercut.

Therefore, from an economics context, national authorities would have to concur that any assessment of an action (should look at terms of the agreement) should focus on market context[57] market outcomes (of a game) as well as market power. At the level of the national authority, there will be the possibility of opening up own initiative parallel procedures in most EU States requiring cooperation between Member State competition authorities. The Commission encourages more cooperation with Member States against a background where an effects based doctrine requires more reliance on economics. Market shares will differ as a threshold across Member States given rise to our 'irrelevance of market share thresholds' but reinforcing the need to use deadweight loss measures to articulate a strong economics defence and exercise the judicial mind in those agreements where product-markets, once separate, now conjoin.

### 3. The 'right' market definition and price abuse

In trying to decide on the 'right' market definition, for example, we may have to move away from the bias towards an exclusively narrow market definition and

---

55 Bill Bishop's Lexecon *Competition Memo*, 12 March 1999.

56 *Vide* Judgement of CFI, 25 March 1999, Merger Case IV/M.619 Gencor/Lonrho.

57 The market shares as concentration indicators are limited—if any usefulness comes from relying on market shares, then one may have to look at entropy measures which focus on market share *redistribution*. A CR4 = 70% tells you absolutely nothing about the underlying market structure or market context, but entropy and *q*-ratio do. The latter measures may be more useful in analysis given (i) the emergence of new challenges for analysis *viz.* connecting markets, internet, telecoms, and (ii) R&D expenditure, cost leadership and innovation as indicators of market performance.

focus on entry and innovation[58] and strategy. In any evaluation of the likely impact of changes to both the legislative and bureaucratic environments, it is imperative in developing competition principles and (therefore new policy directions) that we ask the question: do we have market definition right in this new environment? what method(s) are to be employed to determine price abuse and how do we account for technical progress (while maintaining investment incentives) in measuring consumer welfare?

In particular, the policy environment proposed by the *White Paper* is a move away from *ex-ante* and challenges the use of market definition and the welfare loss measurement in framing competition *ex-post*. Competition law arguably,[59] optimises externality-producing activity that is socially valuable; some offences (for example, cartel price fixing) are socially injurious at any level; their optimal rate is zero. To eradicate such activities efficient law would try to make defendants whole[60] (strips all gain but nothing more). If the defendant expects underdetection, underconviction or inadequate sanctions, recidivist behaviour occurs. The utility loss from being unable to use an asset is not generally the same as the value of lost opportunities to exchange it.

For example, if national authorities know the level of price and hypothesise on the level of competitive price, then a calculation of deadweight loss obtains. The fine equals the amount of deadweight loss, the fine is imposed and the defendant is made whole. Many law-and-economics scholars believe that punitive civil damages have no efficiency rationale beyond correcting for under-deterrence or court error in compensating plaintiffs. There should be an emphasis on criminal sanctions coupled with a set of rules which allow flexibility in the analysis. For example, any presumption of a 'wrong' should be rebutted against a menu of behavioural (game theoretic) characteristics. In other situations—making defendants whole—can show that an expectation of punitive sanctions would advance efficiency.

## V. Concluding comments

### 1. Europe's future: oligopolistically structured[61] industry

In today's business world where cost structure not only varies substantially among firms but are constantly in a state of flux, where excess capacity is a common

---

58 Additionally consider Hammer's example of the horse-drawn-carriage maker: the horse-drawn-carriage maker that should have thought itself as a transport company and was caught out by the car is in fact misleading—there is no particular reason to think that a company that excelled at constructing wooden carriages could adapt to a world of complex automobile manufactures. Rather the carriage company should have identified and capitalised on the strengths of its *operating processes* by diversifying into related industries, for example, by developing wood products and coordinating a supply network.

59 *Vide* McNutt (1998): 'Efficiency in Competition Policy: Expendable Competitors and Making Defendants Whole'. Paper delivered to Strathclyde University Business School/Faculty of Law, 1998.

60 A remedy that makes the plaintiff whole restores all loss and nothing more.

61 *Vide* Special Issue of *European Business Review*, vol. 96, no. 5, 1996, where the author was Guest Editor. *Vide* Tirole (1988): *The Theory of Industrial Organisation*, MIT Press and for policy and

occurrence, and where innovative advances in products and process technology are a matter of competitive reality, it is difficult to understand that process[62] by which firms independently expand output until competitive returns are realised. Dynamic rather than static efficiency has become the paramount aspect of industrial performance today. The publication of the *White Paper* therefore presents an opportunity to re-evaluate the principles of economics underlying European competition policy.

It is worth noting that as Europe's industrial (business) stage assumes the status of oligopoly, there may be increasing support for the arguments advanced by some economists that a measure of price coordination is necessary in an oligopolistically structured industry. Economic theory would have us believe that price coordination is designed to reduce the uncertainty associated with interdependence and there by decrease the likelihood of mutually destructive price competition. If such arguments persist, legislators may have to take cognisance of a view[63] expressed recently:

[T]hat in a perfect, frictionless world, businesses could still meet and fix prices. This would result in technical violation of our competition laws and even in criminal fines. But it could not substantially harm consumer welfare because perfect information among businesses would allow some to quickly enter the price fixed markets and compete away the supra-competitive profits. The competition would soon drive prices down to only an insignificant fraction above the competitive level.

Whatever the views of theorists, competition agencies will continue to have concerns that (price-fixing) mechanisms designed to avoid price warfare can also be used to artificially increase prices (and profit) significantly above the competitive level at the expense of the consumer. To reiterate my view: some offences, particularly cartel price fixing, are socially injurious at any level; their optimal rate is zero.

## 2. Future competition policy

Economic integration need not conflict with moves to safeguard competition. It is a fundamental attribute and driver for change at the Commission and particularly at DG Competition which has responsibility for competition policy. The market context in which an agreement, action or proposed merger occurs is important for analysis. There are alternative measures of market power that may be more appropriate in assessing firm conduct in the future. The national authorities may be better

---

*cont.*
theory *vide* Phlips (1995): *Competition Policy: Game Theoretic Perspectives*, Cambridge University Press. Also various volumes of *European Economic Review* and *International Journal of Industrial Organisation* and *Journal of Industrial Economics*.

62 The process referred to is (perfect) competition, which represents a static equilibrium. Contestable markets and Clarke's workable competition, are more open to embracing non-static equilibrium. Regretably, 'competition' and 'contestable' are so often used interchangeably in competition decisions and Clarke's concept has been confined to the history books.

63 *Vide* Averitt and Lande (1997): 'Consumer Sovereignty: A Unified Theory of Antitrust and Consumer Protection Law' *Antitrust Law Journal*, vol. 65, no. 3, Spring 1997.

equipped than the courts to provide robust economic assessment and analysis. Rather than always informing the Commission of our activities and methodology, it may be a wise move by national authorities, in the emerging federal Europe, to consider the adoption a common set of economic principles. After all the *White Paper* advocates a system not dissimilar to that obtaining in another common market, that of US antitrust. Regretably, the *White Paper* is silent (para 96) on solution to issues of coordination between national authorities and consistency of decision making. The author welcomes the proposals but acknowledges that solutions have to be created if the Commission, national courts and national authorities are co-administering the new rules of competition.

A new Commission, free of the burden of notifications, will be in a strong lead position to take a more active role in merger policy at a time when so many of the largest European undertakings operate in more than one Member State. Arguably, mergers today are not easily assessed by the national competition authorities merely of one Member State, thus requiring the Commission to take jurisdiction. If the vision of the founding fathers is to be realised, some[64] would concede that competition policy will inevitably have to give priority to the imperatives of other Community policies; however, it is difficult to conceive of a single economic market that does not have competition policy as one of its central objectives.

The earlier economic cycle of smaller firms is being replaced by a small number of larger firms across the business/industrial landscape of Europe. European debate on (large) size, on efficiency (as an antitrust defence) and on co-operation (as a *sine qua non* of European firm survival in a global market) may trickle down to become important and decisive national (competition policy) issues. Competition authorities will have to concentrate more on assessments of market outcomes, that is, more or less collusive or non-collusive nature of non-cooperative equilibrium. In other words, firm behaviour can no longer be understood as emerging from the (Stigler-Bain) world but has to be seen as emerging from a more complex world of strategic interaction. Quite frankly, competition authorities will have to embrace new economics and the old chestnut of efficiency (as an antitrust defence) and other issues[65] must be tackled by the Commission and national authorities.

As Disraeli[66] once put it:

Man has deified corn and wine. But not even the Irish or the Chinese have erected temples to tea and potatoes.

---

64 Goyder (1988) alluded to this point many years ago in *EEC Competition Law*, Oxford University Press.

65 To put this in its proper perspective, serious and profound questions of policy may well have to be asked by Member States: do smaller Member States require a national merger policy? do smaller Member States require a national merger policy with(out) a prior notification system? The question of national merger policy is not for this conference; however, when we refer to horizontal agreements, a categorical approach could apply coupled with a higher size threshold and entry test for smaller Member States. Will a trade dimension have to be included in any competition assessment? Do we embrace the standard that harm to competitors is not sufficient to determine whether an action is anticompetitive. And if so, what welfare measures do we adopt to identify harm (to competition)? Is harm to competition the appropriate welfare measure when assessing mergers?

66 Disraeli: 'Coningsby or the New Generation' *New York American Library*, 1962, pp. 134–136.

Competition policy may be the tea and potatoes of our European economic policy; our basic competition principles in an integrating Europe, however, deserve a more rational and expert consideration than they are presently receiving. Therefore there will have to emerge from the Commission, over the next few years, a coherent interpretation of competition principles with community-wide effect. In the interim, national authorities should take up the gauntlet and agree to wed their assessments of mergers, actions and (both horizontal and vertical) agreements to a detailed consideration of strategic behaviour.

# Chapter Six: A UK Perspective on the Europeanisation of National Competition Law

MARGARET BLOOM[1,2]

## I. Introduction

A year ago the Centre for the Law of the European Union at University College London organised a conference on The Europeanisation of UK Competition Law at which I spoke about the OFT's role in the new UK regime. At that time the Act was still only the Competition Bill: Royal Assent was two months later. Between the last conference and this one, much has been achieved in defining and preparing for the new competition regime. Although the preparations and details are not yet complete, it is clear that the Competition Act 1998 introduces a significant Europeanisation of our national law. It will be most interesting to compare, in this conference, our Europeanisation with that of other Member States. In preparing for our new regime the Office of Fair Trading (OFT) has already benefited greatly from the advice and information provided by the European Commission and by other national competition authorities—including those speaking today—who have already adopted Europeanised national competition laws.

As I explained last year, the Competition Act 1998 is the most significant reform of UK competition law for 25 years; that is since the creation of the OFT itself by the Fair Trading Act 1973. In discussing the Europeanisation of UK competition law I shall first consider the close similarity of the new UK regime with the EC regime in the Treaty of Rome (i.e. essentially Arts. 81 and 82) before exploring some of the differences which, nevertheless, exist between the two regimes. I shall then look at the timing and preparations for implementing the Competition Act 1998. Lastly, I shall outline the OFT priorities for making the most effective use of our new Europeanised regime. The mergers regime is essentially unaffected by the new Act. I shall not, therefore, speak about mergers, despite the consultation that is currently being undertaken by DTI on possible proposals for reform.[3]

## II. Similarity of new UK regime with EC regime

The Competition Act 1998 has been drafted so that there will be close conformity with the EC regime. Given that the EC competition rules are directly applicable in the UK where an agreement or conduct may affect trade between Member States, it

---

1 Director of Competition Policy, Office of Fair Trading.

2 The views expressed in this chapter are personal and are not necessarily those of the DGFT.

3 *Mergers: A Consultation Document on Proposals for Reform*, DTI, August 1999.

*J. Rivas and M. Horspool (eds), Modernisation and Decentralisation of EC Competition Law*, 69–78.
© 2000 *Kluwer Law International*.

is clearly desirable for business for the two regimes to be as similar to each other as possible. This is more so given the ease with which the inter-state trade test can be met.[4] Conformity between the two regimes has been achieved in a number of ways in the new Act:

- The wording for the Chapters I and II prohibitions in the Competition Act 1998 follows that of Arts. 81 and 82 very closely. (The exclusion for undertakings entrusted with services of general economic interest is also modelled on Art. 86(2) of the Treaty of Rome.)
- Section 60 ensures that EC principles are imported; hence the words are inter-preted in accordance with European jurisprudence. I shall discuss this section, which is a particularly important section of the new Act, in more detail below.
- The provisions for parallel exemptions in the Act ensure that the EC block exemptions and individual exemptions granted by the European Commission have automatic effect under the domestic prohibition. This is so in that even if a particular agreement does not affect trade between Member States, it still enjoys the benefit of a parallel exemption if it satisfies the terms of a European block exemption.
- Agreements notified to the European Commission automatically obtain provi-sional immunity from financial penalties under the national law, just as they do under EC law.

In addition, European Court of Justice (ECJ) cases, such as *Leur-Bloem* and *Bronner*, have established conclusively that references may be made to the ECJ on the interpretation of Arts. 81 and 82 where a domestic court or tribunal is consider-ing corresponding issues under Chapters I and II of the new Act. The Competition Commission's appeal tribunals are expected to be eligible to use this Art. 234 pro-cedure as tribunals. Art. 234 references by either the Competition Commission or national courts will, no doubt, be important in establishing precedents in future.

## 1. Section 60

Section 60 states that, as far as possible, questions arising under the Act must be dealt with in a manner that is consistent with the treatment of corresponding ques-tions arising in Community law. The section refers to the need to have regard to any relevant differences—an obvious example being that Arts. 81 and 82 are part of a Treaty with a single market objective. In addition to the requirement that the prin-ciples laid down in the EC Treaty and judgments of the ECJ are to be followed, those taking decisions in the UK under the Act must have regard to relevant deci-sions or statements of the European Commission. In this way, the Act essen-tially imports 35 years of EC jurisprudence. We understand that other Member States—for example Italy and Denmark—have comparable provisions, although by

---

4 Whether following the recent *Bagnasco* judgment in Cases C-215/216/96 (1999) ECR I-0135, the European Commission will be rather more inclined in some cases to conclude that there is no appreciable effect, actual or potential, on trade between Member States remains to be seen.

requiring the UK authorities to have regard to statements of the European Commission, rather than just Commission decisions and judgements of the ECJ, the Competition Act probably goes further. The formula Statement of the Commission is limited to those Statements which have the authority of the European Commission, such as, the *Annual Report on Competition Policy*, comfort letters which have been preceded by a notice in the Official Journal under Art. 19(3) of Regulation 17/62, Commission decisions and Commission notices such as those giving guidance on the treatment of joint ventures under Art. 81.

One implication of section 60 is that the Competition Act should not be read as standard UK legislation. Its meaning needs to be interpreted in line with European jurisprudence, for example, the words "effect on competition" in section 2 must be read as meaning "appreciable effect on competition". Another example is that references to products in section 9 should be read as meaning goods and services. Section 60 does not import the detailed Commission procedures. The procedural rules of the Director General of Fair Trading (DGFT), though, may not depart from the EC high level principles such as the principle of fairness in administrative action and the principle of proportionality. However, in considering these high level principles, account needs to be taken of the fact that the appeal system under the Act is fuller than under EC law. Therefore, in considering whether the Act gives effect to the high level principles, both the rules of the DGFT and of the Competition Commissions appeals tribunals need to be considered as a whole. In practice, the DGFT's procedures are largely modelled on those of the European Commission, with some simplifications to improve some unduly cumbersome procedures while ensuring procedures remain fair. The OFT procedures for potential infringement cases include access to the non-confidential parts of the file, the issuing of a statement of objections and the ability for parties to make oral, as well as, written representations. A statement of objections will set out the facts on which the DGFT relies, the conclusions that he draws from those facts, a legal assessment, the action he proposes to take and his reasons for such action. It will also attach a list of all the documents in the DGFT's file. A party may request a meeting with the OFT to make oral representations to supplement its written submission, if it wishes to, and may be asked questions if appropriate.

## III. Some significant differences

Despite the close similarity between the two regimes there are some differences in the wording and in the relevant policies. The main differences are, I suggest, various exclusions in the new Act, namely the implications of the DGFT's guidance on appreciable effects, the DGFT's policy on leniency and the concurrent powers for sector regulators. Before discussing these in some detail, I should refer to various other differences.

First, as mentioned above, the appeal system in the UK regime is different from that under EC law. Arguably, this is a particularly significant difference that should be considered in more detail. However, given that the procedures for the appeals tribunal have not yet been finalised, substantive discussion of this difference could be premature. At this stage, it may nevertheless be helpful if I summarise the position.

Under the Act, an appeal will be on the merits of the case and the appeal tribunals will be able to substitute their discretion (e.g. in the grant of an exemption) for that of the DGFT. This contrasts with the EC position where the Court of First Instance is confined, at least in theory, to reviewing Commission decisions on judicial review-type grounds. In addition, a wider range of third parties will be able to appeal under national law than is possible under EC law.

In contrast to EC law, it is possible for any UK exemption to be backdated to the date of the agreement. The European Commission can, of course, only provide retroactive exemptions for vertical agreements and a few others. Indeed, the amendment to Regulation 17 to allow retroactive exemptions for vertical agreements was only introduced earlier this year. Arguably, the possibility of backdating any UK exemption is also a significant difference. The Commission consider that the recent amendment to Regulation 17 will materially reduce the number of notifications. Similarly, we consider the possibility to backdate any exemption under UK law will reduce notifications. If so, the wider scope for backdating under UK law is a significant and valuable difference.

The other, less significant differences which I wish to mention are as follows:

- Legal privilege covers a wider class of documents under the UK regime, including advice by in-house counsel.
- There is a provision in the Act for limited immunity from penalties for small and medium sized enterprises. Price fixing agreements are excluded from this limited immunity.
- Perhaps, not strictly a difference between national legislation and EC law, is the fact that the Act does not provide for direct Art. 81(1) or 82 powers for the DGFT. Currently, eight out of the 15 Member States have such direct powers. However, generally they have been little used in practice. The Spanish competition authorities appear to have been the most active in using their direct powers. In some Member States, at least, one of the reasons for using the powers has been where action could not be taken under national law because, for example, of an exclusion.
- The final example in my list concerns the fact that, subject to agreement of the Secretary of State, there will be fees for notifications for guidance and decisions. These fees will cover the full cost of the work involved in providing guidance (expected to be between £3000 and £6000) or a decision (expected to be between £10,000 and £16,000). The latter will involve considerably more work than the former—not least because of the consultation involved—and hence will bear significantly higher fees.

Let me now turn to considering in some detail the main differences that I identified above i.e. exclusions, guidance on appreciable effect, leniency and concurrent powers.

## 1. Exclusions

As I mentioned, there are various exclusions in the Act which do not exist in European law. All those agreements with directions under section 21(2) of the

Restrictive Trade Practices Act are permanently excluded from the new Act unless the agreements are materially varied. This is a welcome exclusion which both removes the need for the OFT to examine a large number of harmless agreements and for business to notify them. Over 6000 agreements have been given section 21(2) directions since 1989. Two other important and welcome exclusions are those for vertical agreements and land agreements. These exclusions are also aimed at ensuring that neither the resources of the OFT nor business are wasted on examining harmless agreements. For these three exclusions—which only apply to Chapter I— there is a claw-back provision available to the DGFT. Under this, if the DGFT considers that an agreement will, if not excluded, infringe the Chapter I prohibition and he is not likely to grant it an unconditional individual exemption, he may give a direction to disapply the exclusion. Another important difference between national law and EC law, which is material in relation to the vertical agreements exclusion, is the retention of the complex monopoly powers under the Fair Trading Act 1973. These powers can be used where, for example, a network of vertical agreements in a market has a cumulative adverse effect on competition. The powers—which are an abuse control regime—enable the DGFT to refer a market to the Competition Commission for examination where it appears to him that there are grounds for believing that 25% or more of the supply of specified goods or services are provided by businesses who so conduct their affairs, by agreement or otherwise, as to prevent, restrict or distort competition. They have, for example, recently been used for references of motor cars and supermarkets to the Competition Commission.

## 2. Appreciable effect

In order to reduce unnecessary notifications of harmless agreements, the OFT guidelines state that the DGFT considers that where parties to an agreement have a market share which does not exceed 25%, it is unlikely that their agreement will have an appreciable effect on competition unless it involves price fixing, market sharing or it is part of a network of agreements with a cumulative effect on competition. The latter agreements will, indeed, mostly be vertical ones and benefit from the above exclusion in the first place. Parties are advised not to notify agreements unless they have an appreciable effect on competition. The advice on market shares does not, of course, imply that those agreements where the parties have more than 25% of the market will necessarily have an appreciable effect on competition or need to be notified.

## 3. Leniency policy

The OFT consider that the combination of the various exclusions, parallel exemptions and advice against notifying most agreements with a market share of 25% or less means that the vast majority of agreements are not affected by the Chapter I prohibition. Or to rephrase this, only those agreements with a potentially serious effect on competition are caught. Notably, this includes cartels where we would, of course, welcome notifications! Given the obvious reluctance of parties to make such notifications, an effective leniency policy is essential to stimulate whistleblowers seeking amnesty.

As mentioned above, another area where there is a significant difference between the national and EC regimes relates to the policy on leniency. The OFT is much aware of the success of the Department of Justice (DoJ) approach whereby the first member of a cartel to report the illegal activity is granted amnesty provided that various conditions are met. Amnesty is automatic if there is no pre-existing investigation. The other conditions include the requirement that the company was not the leader in or originator of the cartel and did not coerce another party to participate in the illegal activity. Amnesty may still be automatic if cooperation begins after the investigation is underway. The DoJ's provision of automatic amnesty was introduced in August 1993. At that time around one company a year was coming forward under the then existing leniency agreements. This initially rose to one a month under the new policy and has now reached two companies a month. The stimulus of competition is having a dramatic effect! We plan to introduce a similar leniency policy and are consulting on this as part of the consultation on the guidance on penalties required under section 38 of the Act.[5] Even with the very weak powers of investigation in our current legislation, we uncover a continuing number of cartels: nine over the past 18 months. As do the European Commission and other national authorities. The DoJ have uncovered international cartels covering a broad spectrum of commerce. Clearly, many, if not all, these cartels are in operation in the UK. For example, 21 out of the 26 companies which the DoJ have fined $10 million or more in recent years were not US companies—the majority were European. I understand that some of the European capitals are favourite meeting places for international cartels that avoid meeting, if at all possible, in the US.

The consultation on the guidance on penalties also covers the steps to be followed by the DGFT when determining the level of a financial penalty. In preparing this guidance we have had regard to the Commission *Guidelines on the method of setting fines imposed pursuant to Art. 15(2) of Regulation no. 17 and Art. 65(5) of the ECSC Treaty.* The Secretary of State has announced that the maximum penalty that may be imposed will be 10% of the UK turnover of the infringing undertaking for each year of the infringement, up to a maximum of three years. This compares with a maximum of 10% of world turnover in the preceding business year under the EC regime.

## 4. Concurrent powers for sector regulators

The last significant difference that I will discuss concerns the concurrent powers for the regulators for telecommunications, gas, electricity, water and rail. In addition, concurrent powers are likely to be extended to the Civil Aviation Authority. In comparison with other countries, it is unusual for regulators to have competition powers; although there are a few exceptions in some other jurisdictions, almost entirely in banking and telecommunications. However, the UK sector regulators are also unusual in the strength of their expertise and their current regulatory powers. Their licensing regimes include powers to address market power which overlap with Chapter II powers. With a number of bodies able to make decisions under the new

---

5 *Formal Consultation Draft on Competition Act 1998: Director General of Fair Trading's guidance as to the appropriate amount of a penalty*, OFT, August 1999.

Act, consistency is clearly paramount. Hence, there are a number of mechanisms either in the Act or developed subsequently, which will ensure consistency of decisions. These include the fact that section 60 applies equally to the regulators as to the DGFT, the guidelines on the Act and procedural rules are common to the regulators and DGFT, also the appeal system is common with all the appeals going to the appeal tribunals of the Competition Commission. In addition, joint training in preparation for the new regime is taking place for OFT and regulators' staff. The OFT chaired Concurrency Working Party, which has been overseeing the preparation of the guidelines and rules, will continue and play a significant role in ensuring a consistency of approach in individual cases.

## IV. Timing and preparations

The new Act obtained Royal Assent on 9 November 1998 which was the start of a transitional period running up to 1 March 2000 when the new prohibitions will start. The transitional arrangements continue after that, as, with a few exceptions, agreements made in the interim period between 9 November 1998 and 1 March 2000 are excluded from the Chapter 1 prohibition until 1 March 2001. A similar one year exclusion applies to agreements which were not caught by the Restrictive Trade Practices Act, for example, because only one party accepted restrictions. A few agreements (various utility agreements, agreements already found by the Restrictive Practices Court not to be contrary to the public interest, and a few other special categories) have a five rather than one year exclusion.

In preparation for implementation on 1 March 2000, the OFT is recruiting additional staff, training staff and undertaking a major education programme for business. Recruitment of additional staff is likely to continue well into 2000 as the OFT expands to meet full implementation of the new regime in 2001. Staff working on competition policy are expected to increase from around 150 to around 200. New recruits will be either lawyers or economists by expertise, have experience as investigation officers or have relevant experience from working in a competition authority. The training programme for OFT and sector regulator staff started in May 1999. This is a rolling six months programme covering economics, law and competition policy. Staff are required to pass the assessment tests as part of the training. This training is on top of the university degree that is held by many members of staff.

## 1. Business education programme

The business education programme is important in ensuring that business prepares for the new Europeanised regime both so that firms refrain from anti-competitive behaviour and those suffering from such behaviour are alerted to the opportunity to complain to the OFT. The programme includes the production of guidelines on the application and enforcement of the legislation, short explanatory booklets aimed at a more general guidance, OFT speakers at seminars and conferences, regional business advice open days, an explanatory leaflet on the Act for all firms on the VAT register, a video Compliance Matters showing an on-site investigation, a radio tape, enquiry line (0207-211 8989) and material on the OFT website (oft.gov.uk).

## 2. Guidelines

Around 20 guidelines are currently planned. Of these, the nine core guidelines (covering *The Major Provisions, The Chapter I Prohibition, The Chapter II Prohibition, Market Definition, Powers of Investigation, Concurrent Application to Regulated Industries, Transitional Arrangements, Enforcement, and Trade Associations, Professions and Self-Regulated Bodies*) were published in their final version in March 1999. The Act, rightly, requires a formal consultation on drafts of the guidelines. The consultation process has been most valuable and the OFT is grateful to all those who have contributed to it. The consultation is complete on another five guidelines covering *Assessment of Market Power, Assessment of Individual Agreements and Conduct, Mergers and Ancillary Restraints, Application of the Competition Act in the Telecommunications Sector and Application in the Water and Sewerage Sectors*. The first three are expected to be published in early October. There are another six guidelines in preparation covering services of General Economic Interest (i.e. equivalent to Art. 86(2)), *Application in the Energy Sectors, Application in the Railway Sector, Land Agreements, Vertical Agreements and Restraints and Intellectual Property Rights*. The guidelines on land, vertical agreements and intellectual property rights await the details of the statutory instruments for the exclusion of land and vertical agreements.

## 3. Business awareness

The short, explanatory booklets mentioned above, are largely aimed at small and medium sized businesses. The first booklet *What your business needs to know* is a general introduction to the new Act. It was published in the Spring of 1999. A booklet explaining how to complain about anti-competitive practices will be published nearer to the start of the new regime. Another booklet which gives advice on compliance programmes How *your business can achieve compliance* has just been published. Others will follow. In terms of speakers, OFT staff have addressed approaching 200 events organised by trade associations, chambers of commerce, law firms and commercial conference organisers. As a basis against which to assess our performance in educating business about the new Act, a survey of business awareness was conducted for us in February and March 1999. This showed that 77% of key business managers in small and medium sized firms had no awareness of the new legislation, 21% did not know very much and just 2% had detailed knowledge. Surveys will be conducted in Spring 2000 and 2001 against a target to improve business awareness.

## V. OFT priorities

The central objective of the OFT in implementing the new regime is to concentrate resources on serious anti-competitive practices. This is a similar objective to that of the European Commission in their *White Paper on Modernisation of the Rules*

*Implementing Arts. 85 and 86[6] of the EC Treaty.* Clearly it must be right for both the Commission and national authorities to be able to use their resources to produce maximum economic benefit for their taxpayers. This requires appropriate laws and procedures. Perhaps the conference next year should consider how Europeanisation has moved a stage further with the development of the modernisation proposals from the Commission. A particular angle could be how the reforms will ensure that national authorities and the Commission can, and do, together address serious anti-competitive behaviour. Meanwhile I should like to conclude by outlining how we propose to do this with our new regime.

As I have already indicated, the OFT is much aware of the extent of cartel activity which current UK legislation leaves largely untouched. The new regime, modelled on European competition law, provides the OFT with effective powers to deal with damaging anti-competitive behaviour. For the first time we will have effective powers of investigation, fines and other sanctions such as voidness of agreements infringing the Chapter I prohibition and interim measures. Hence, as part of the business education programme we are mounting a campaign '*Do complain. Do not notify*'. Complaints are the best source of information about anti-competitive behaviour. These can, for example, provide evidence of refusals to supply for no apparent reason, of a competitor who has suggested setting prices or of an anti-competitive supply agreement being forced by a powerful company on a weaker one. The new Act is an opportunity for businesses which have been suffering from anti-competitive behaviour. The priorities of the OFT will be:

- combating cartels and other damaging anti-competitive behaviour. Complaints and whistleblowers will be important;
- publishing reasoned decisions which establish precedents. This is in addition to the 35 years of EC jurisprudence imported through section 60;
- processing efficiently the few notifications which genuinely need decision or guidance.

As explained earlier, we consider that the vast majority of agreements will not be caught, in practice, by the legislation. Hence few agreements will genuinely need to be notified for decision or guidance. Where agreements are caught, parties will need to consider carefully whether to notify the OFT or the European Commission. Given the wide interpretation of the scope of European legislation in respect to agreements which may affect trade between Member States, many parties will have the choice of whether to notify OFT or the Commission. Dual notifications are strongly discouraged. A notification to Brussels gives the parties provisional immunity against both EC and national law. A notification to the OFT has no effect in EC law. Similarly, an EC exemption, if obtained, applies in national law. In relation to comfort letters from the Commission, the OFT guidelines state that the DGFT will not normally depart from the Commissions assessment and, if intending to do so, would first discuss with the Commission. Lastly, despite the recent amendment to Regulation 17, it is still not possible for the Commission to give retroactive

---

6  Now Arts. 81 and 82.

exemptions for a significant proportion of agreements; whereas this is possible for all agreements under UK national law so that notification can be delayed until, and if, a need for exemption arises, for example, during an action to enforce an agreement. Both the European Commission and the OFT equally discourage notifications. However, where parties are unsure about whom to notify, we are happy to offer informal advice based on informal discussion.

## VI. Conclusion

The UK has waited a long time for Europeanisation of our national competition law. The importance of this Europeanisation is in introducing effective competition law in the UK. The new UK regime has been carefully prepared with some, well thought out, differences between the UK and European regimes. In addition, the implementation arrangements have been thoroughly planned. The UK authorities are determined to make effective use of these new powers to root out damaging anti-competitive behaviour.

# Chapter Seven: Official Written Response of France to the White Paper*

## PIERRE CHAMBU[1]

This document aims to define the French position on the White Paper adopted on 28 April 1999. At this stage, the French Authorities wish to specify the reasons why the general direction taken by the Commission is appropriate and to formulate our commentary on the mechanisms of the planned reforms, while focusing on the main measures proposed.[2]

## I. Regarding the principle of a system of legal exception

With reference to the set of agreements and practices relevant to Arts. 81 and 82 of the Treaty, it is advisable to replace the administrative system of prior authorisation established in the early 1960s with an *ex post* decentralised control process. In view of the main considerations to be taken into account, the following are our comments on the establishment of a system of legal exemption.

### 1. Effectiveness in protecting competition will be reinforced

1.1. Notifications are not an effective means of surveillance of the market

The White Paper rightly shows this in a pragmatic way. This is confirmed by a detailed analysis of the Commission's decisions:

—Dangerous agreements falling under the prohibitions are not being notified.
—Experience shows that the useful practices used in the enforcement of Arts. 81 and 82 (prohibitions and decisions imposing commitments) could be accomplished without the notification system, either by initiating *ex officio* procedures (if need be after an investigation) or by dealing with complaints.
—The notification system, dealt with on an administrative level, seems therefore to foster a poor allocation of resources.

---

* This is an Unofficial English translation of the French position.
1 Direction Générale de la Consommation, de la Concurrence et de la Répression des Fraudes, France.
2 An appendix is provided for any useful purpose on the French position regarding options rejected by the Commission.

*J. Rivas and M. Horspool (eds), Modernisation and Decentralisation of EC Competition Law*, 79–87.
© 2000 *Kluwer Law International*.

## 1.2. The legal exception system will help assure a greater effectiveness in enforcing the rules on competition

The proposed reforms will not weaken the deterrent effect of the basic prohibitions decreed by Art. 81.[3] On the contrary, it will reinforce them by permitting a better allocation of the Commission's administrative resources, which will have a beneficial effect on *ex post* controls, keeping the market in line more effectively.

## 2. Coherence in the application of the rules will be guaranteed

2.1. A decentralised application of Art. 81(3) is possible

In any case, the requirement that the application of Community law on competition be coherent does not require that the Commission have a monopoly in the application of Art. 81(3), where abundant jurisprudence has set out the terms of its enforcement:

—The fundamental principle of the primacy of Community law is established in the area of competition.
—The fundamental institutional mechanisms which guarantee this primacy are already in place (removal by the Commission of a case from the jurisdiction of a national authority, references for preliminary rulings).

The choice made in 1962 for the Commission to have a monopoly on the application of Art. 81(3) is historically outdated. It was made within a context where all the Member States did not have competition authorities, and it was tied to the solution adopted on the procedural level (administrative authorisation).

Most of all, we were not yet able to appreciate the strong centralising affects this monopoly would have on the regulation of agreements. (It was only afterwards that jurisprudence empowered Art. 81 with a large field of application, almost as large as the national law because it even extends to cover practices where the effects might be limited to a local segment of the national geographic market.)

Art. 82, which calls for no less a coherent application, was directly applicable for the national jurisdictions from the very beginning, and then gradually for a growing number of national competition authorities.[4] Whether it has to do with its technical nature (demarcation of the market, characterising a dominant position) or the economic consequences implicated within the internal market, its execution is neither easier nor less important than that of Art. 81(3). The same applies for other dispositions of the Treaty, also directly applicable (notably those pertaining to free movement).

---

3 This system does not transform the regulating of agreements into a mere control of abuses, permitting only to prohibit for the future (a certain practice only becomes illicit after the date the infraction is established).
4 The same as for Art. 81(1).

## 2.2. A decentralised application of Art. 81(3) is desirable

The monopoly of the Commission in the application of Art. 81(3) carries the consequence of a case allocation, which is excessively centralised and this is a factor in the creation of legal inefficiency and uncertainty. In addition, it deters the national authorities from enforcing automatically Art. 81 (causing their jurisdiction to be compromised) in many cases where internal law instead is applied.

As such this monopoly, far from guaranteeing coherence, could actually be an obstacle to the process of harmonisation, which is necessary for the consolidation of the internal market. In effect, every time it acts to take into account the efficiencies induced by certain restrictions of competition, it perpetuates the risks of divergence between the national jurisprudence and that of the Community.

## 3. Legal certainty will not be weakened

Requiring a satisfactory level of legal certainty need not force us to maintain a system of notification.

## 3.1. At present there exists a well established body of rules

By freeing them from responsibility, the notification system fosters the notion that corporations cannot evaluate their own agreements, a situation that rarely occurs. In the early 1960s, while jurisprudence and decision making were still embryonic, such a diagnosis may have been based on objective arguments. However these arguments have quickly become less and less solid, and today this diagnosis is largely outdated. The Commission closes out almost all the procedures of notification by comfort letters[5] without intervening, which shows that the majority of businesses that provide notification have no real need for the Commission's guardianship to be able to conform to the rules on competition. Giving up these letters would bring with it no legal uncertainty for those that continue to follow the rules. There is no reason that agreements which are today notified, which have never been prohibited, might be annulled in the future because the substantial law will not have been modified. The fear of a dramatic increase in litigation related difficulties is therefore not well founded.

## 3.2. There are elements which help reinforce legal certainty

It is worth mentioning the technique of exemption regulations and guidelines. For those businesses that do not hold a powerful market position, the evolution towards an economic approach will lead to a simplification of matters and legal certainty. The adoption of a system of legal exception would enhance the positive effects of this approach. At the present time many agreements falling under the scope of Art. 81(1), but indeed complying with Art. 81(3), are not being notified. This happens mostly with small or medium sized businesses for which notification presents a high cost. Their legal certainty situation would be clearly improved. The fact that

---

5 Which, furthermore, are not opposable in the courts.

the Commission has a monopoly on exemptions sometimes provokes co-contractors to invoke the law on competition in order to have an agreement declared invalid for the sole reason that it had not been notified, regardless of whether or not there existed any threat to competition. The direct applicability of Art. 81(3), related to the elimination of notifications, will render this type of action pointless.

3.3. It is possible to correct areas of uncertainty by non-bureaucratic means

Certain areas of uncertainty remain, notably in the case of market power, where the law regarding competition calls specifically for a case by case approach. These do not occur in frequent number. Concerning the immense majority of agreements that are not covered by a block exemption (medium market share but over a certain threshold, conditions for exemption not met, etc.) the ability to predict compliance with the rules of competition is already high and will continue to grow.

From a technical point of view, the few situations which might need legitimate questioning do not justify the maintenance of an anticipatory and systematic control:

—Very often today we find that when agreements which are notified present problems it is mainly a question of making adjustments, such as in the modification of certain clauses, so that the degree to which competition is restricted might be precisely fine-tuned according to the desired objective. This could be done *ex post*. A possible *a priori* intervention by the Commission, to clarify a question, might be conceived of. *But its response should be adapted to each particular case.* It could be the case that a formal *ex ante* clarification might be necessary concerning the law regarding competition (and the White Paper does foresee this possibility). However, this only concerns a few cases.
—The implementation of Art. 81(3) also leads to ask for undertakings from parties to an agreement. To this end it might be possible to rely therein on *ex post* regulatory mechanisms (opening of a procedure *ex officio*, adopting a decision with undertakings) which would enable a conditional approval of the agreements. In any case, an anticipatory dialogue with the authorities on competition is possible.

## II. Regarding the conditions of the reform

### 1. It is advisable to clarify the issue of case allocation

Maintaining a system of shared authority and flexible allocation is advisable in the case of agreements or abuses of dominant position. The general orientation of the Commission's planning (determining the most appropriate authority to protect competition by measure of its access to evidence, its capacity to resolve the case and the existence of a particular interest for the EC) constitutes a good starting point.

In any case, the actual transparency of case allocation would be necessary in order for the plan of action to be effective. It is indispensable that the reorganisation pursuant to the notice of 15 October 1997 on the cooperation of the Commission with the national competition authorities be carried out as a priority along with the reform of Regulation no. 17, as high upstream in the process as is possible, and within the framework of wide consultation with the economic world. As a first priority, the group of experts should specifically consider and delve into all the aspects (operational and legal) of this matter, which is dotted with certain complexities. It should notably evaluate the optimal level of specification for each of the allocation criteria, with special attention to the geographic polarisation of the effects.

*The French authorities insist particularly on the importance of clarifying the specifications regarding jurisdiction of the Commission and the national authorities.*

## 2. Coherence should be based on simple and non-bureaucratic mechanisms

2.1. Cooperation within the network

An obligation to inform the Commission is needed on the part of the national competition authorities when applying Community law. The purpose is to avoid resorting to corrective mechanisms (which remain indispensable) to guarantee a coherent application of this law.

The level of information supplied to the Commission should be sufficient to allow for a useful response (consultation within the Consultative Committee and when lacking, auto-referral). It should be the same for whichever State member is concerned. The principle of a 'due hearing' requires that the information provided and the collaboration within the Consultative Committee be instilled with sufficient guarantees regarding transparency. Finally, the methods for informing the Commission should reject any bureaucratic burden within the network itself.

The notice of 15 October 1997 provides for supplying information to the Commission on a purely optional basis after 'initiating any proceedings', a terminology which lends itself to different interpretations according to the procedural regulations of each individual authority. Within the framework of mandatory information, this terminology may not be precise enough to assure the homogeneity of the information supplied to the Commission by the national authorities.

The French authorities do not intend to analyse this matter in detail here, but rather request the Commission to ask the task force to define an adequate '*modus operandi*'.

2.2. *A priori* decisions attesting to the validity of a practice

In theory this mechanism, which aims to provide the Commission with an additional means to define European policy on competition with respect to matters of great importance, is an advisable approach. It could be adopted on the condition that within its mechanisms, it does not act to create a new source of notifications. This risk should therefore be set aside by means of an appropriate drafting of a text, taking into account the pertinent ECJ jurisprudence. Otherwise another solution might be studied (for example, the publication of opinions). *The objective which should be sought is to formulate good technical solutions in order that the Commission might find itself able to approve a priori certain activities when this seems indispensable if a new uncontrollable source of notifications is to be avoided.*

### 2.3. Jurisdictional authorities

#### 2.3.1. Cooperation

Coherence in the application of Art. 81(3) on the part of national jurisdictions will fundamentally rest on references for preliminary rulings. This coherence will be reinforced by the development of cooperation with the Commission which, although provided for by the present texts, has remained to this day fairly limited, taking into account the exclusive jurisdiction of the Commission over the application of Art. 81(3).

The notice of 13 February 1993 sets up a flexible cooperation between the Commission and the national jurisdictions. This document should be modified to take into account the elimination of the notification procedure, but it is recommendable that the principle of flexibility in this cooperation be maintained. Much in the same way, the direct intervention of the Commission on the hearings in national procedures, would be a burdensome and costly solution. One alternative might be for the Commission to suggest to the Member States the adoption of a mechanism of the type provided for in France by Art. 56 of the Order of 1 December 1986, permitting the national authorities, if it be the case, to relay an opinion of the Commission. Here also, the establishment of an obligation on the part of the national jurisdictions to inform the Commission on cases where Community law was applied would place on them a heavy and useless bureaucratic burden. The impact of such an obligation would be very different from that which it would have over the authorities on competition, taking into account the very high number of contractual litigation under which the laws on competition can be invoked incidentally. It seems better to leave it to the courts to decide in their own deliberations when a consultation with the Commission might be called for.

#### 2.3.2. Specialisation

The specialisation of jurisdictions assigned for the application of the law on competition can be studied, as a complementary measure in the adoption of a system of legal exception. A similar solution is already in operation within one Member State.[6] We can recall the existence of a similar disposition in Regulation 40/94 of 20 December 1993 on the EC brand names. Art. 91 of this regulation specifies that for the disputes over falsification and the validity of EC brand names *'The Member States shall designate … as limited a number as possible of national courts and tribunals of first and second instance.'*

### 3. The exchange of confidential information should imperatively be protected by procedural guarantees

The exchange of confidential data between the Commission and the national authorities is as necessary for a proper allocation of cases as it is for the cooperation which is indispensable in a coherent application of Community regulations.

---

6 Germany.

The proposition of the White Paper is fundamentally acceptable. Nevertheless, the French authorities express a reservation of the right to examine the exact definition of the procedural guarantees which will be planned. An obligation should be decreed not to divulge anything to third parties with the only exception being the respect for its need as part of a defense (access for businesses being questioned in a proceeding to elements retained about them, when their own sentencing is at risk). The discussion cannot proceed on this point without examining the actual formulations or text that the Commission will propose. The entire group of procedural guarantees should be provided for in the regulation of the Council, and it should be directly applicable to avoid any heterogeneity between the Member States. It would be advisable also to study attentively the specific questions that the economic world might formulate on the subject.

### 4. Joint ventures call for specific measures

The application of the concentration regulation only to joint ventures of partial production is advisable. In fact, for this category of business, the efficiency of an *ex post* control is unsure, for reasons similar to those in the case of mergers and acquisitions. The integration of productive functions and the intensity of the capital involved which characterise these cooperative operations can create a situation of '*fait accompli*' difficult to put into question *a posteriori*.

Those joint ventures of partial productive activity which remain under the system of legal exception (for example under the sphere of R&D) should nevertheless benefit from a special effort on the level of the predictability of the rules of competition. Parallel to the reform of Regulation no. 17, it is desirable for the Commission to take the initiatives in that which concerns these operations. *Notably, the French authorities believe it is advisable to provide for an anticipatory approval in cases involving investments which are heavy and not easily reversed.* A close collaboration among the Member States seems indispensable in order to gather information on experiences with different mechanisms which should be mobilised (regulations on exemption, organisational guidelines, individual explicit decisions) and the clarifications required. This cooperation could be introduced in the framework of a re-examination of the rules regarding horizontal agreements.

### 5. Judiciary control of investigations should remain national

The White Paper's proposal of a centralisation of judicial control of checks raises some reservations both on the practical and judicial levels.

The rules regarding jurisdiction as foreseen by the Treaty do not permit assigning to a court of EC jurisdiction (ECJC or CFIEC) the power to authorise the Commission to place into effect certain prerogatives of the type which the States use in the application of Art. 14(6) of Regulation no. 17 when providing assistance to the Commission.

Most of all, independently of a hypothetical judicial mandate for the purpose of bypassing an opposition, the assistance lent by the national authorities to the Commission, including when it takes place within the framework of Art. 14(3), is advisable from an operational point of view. *It should therefore not be weakened.*

The proposal of the White Paper lays the basis for a strong centralisation of the judicial authorisation of investigations. The practical justification put forward by the White Paper to back up this proposal (to guarantee the simultaneous and coherent execution of checks) is expressed succinctly. The French authorities believe it is desirable that the Commission dispose of the necessary means to exercise effective *ex post* regulation, while respecting institutional balances. At this stage, the French authorities note that the Commission has not fully disclosed the difficulties that the use of Art. 14 of Regulation no. 17 may create, and which in any case would not be known to justify a solution as centralised as that mentioned by the White Paper.

## III. Conclusion

The above observations on the mechanisms of the reform do not compromise future complementary remarks which the French authorities reserve the right to make on one precise point or another. The French authorities deem indispensable that an expert task force pursue its work on the mechanisms of reform on the basis of a draft of proposed regulation which would then be sent to the Council. In matters regarding the allocation of cases, it would be equally desirable for the work to be undertaken based on a written document.

## Appendix

### Subject: rejected options

Decentralisation of the system of exemptions

Maintaining a system of notifications combined with a decentralisation is not a pertinent alternative. This solution would not reduce the total number of notifications and to the contrary poses the risk of increasing the volume. It would envision a very bureaucratic system, juxtaposing 15 national offices and a Community office, within which the allocation of cases will undoubtedly raise problems.

Under this proposal businesses would have the ability to take the initiative of requesting a national derogation from the Art. 81(1) prohibition principle. In this way the system would structurally carry the risk of non-uniform enforcement of Art. 81(3), which would be of grave consequence and surely lead to conflicting relations within the core of the network. The problem of a too lenient enforcement of Art. 81(3) is a much more delicate matter to resolve in the case of decentralising notifications as opposed to the case of a system of legal exception. In the first case, it would be the corporations themselves, desiring a derogation, who would activate the system. They could look for the 'office' that would be expected to treat them more favourably. The probability that the Commission would deem it necessary to invoke its right to have the case handed over is rather high. In the second case, the corporations that take the decision to refer a matter to one authority or another would be the complainants, trying to obtain a restraint and in that sense opposed to the positive application of Art. 81(3). Moreover, the declaratory nature of positive decisions limits the consequences of contradictory solutions. While the Commission accepts a complaint initially rejected by a national authority, the condemnation would produce its effects fully and immediately because it does not go against a national constitutive decision.

Lightening of procedures

Another option consists of maintaining the monopoly on exemption of the Commission, by lightening at the outset the procedural rules applicable to notifications. But this measure would not be the type of action that could correct the problem of volume posed by the need to administratively manage this control, notably from the perspective of enlargement. It would therefore result in a lack of effectiveness for the policy of European competition, something that cannot be accepted.

Reduction of the field of application of Art. 81(1)

The White Paper emphasises that limiting the flow of notifications by means of an effort to reduce the field of application of Art. 81(1) would be an unsure option, taking into account the uncertainties that the jurisprudence of the Court has handed over regarding this possibility.

The Commission utilises on rare occasions the practical technique of the rule of reason, where a highly extensive conception prevails in its decisions when evaluating an agreement under the angle of Art. 81(1) (assessment of competitive aspects). On the other hand, it is true that the Commission has recourse in a reasoning which is in reality very similar when applying Art. 81(3) (economic assessment). That creative application of the rule of reason at the Community level should be properly placed in perspective with relation to the coexistence of both Community law and national law regarding competition. The ECJ could be hesitating to commit itself to a tendency to a wider application of the rule of reason in its American interpretation (competitive summary), if only to avoid the risk of weakening the primacy of Community law in reducing the space within which it applies itself (field of application of Art. 81(1). In any case it is evident that the adoption of a system of legal exception is, in today's state of jurisprudence, a much more certain solution for effectively re-directing the activity of the Commission towards *ex post* control.

# Chapter Eight: The German View

MARTINA MÜLLER*

The Bundeskartellamt has been in favour of decentralisation for many years and we apply Arts. 81(1) and 82 of the EC Treaty as far as possible. We therefore greatly welcome the proposal by the Commission to decentralise European competition law. However, there are certain differences between the approach of the Commission and that of the Bundeskartellamt. The prevalent difference concerns one of the main features of the White Paper, namely the change from a notification system to a system of legal exception from the application of Art. 81(3). I would prefer the notification system to remain. In Germany we also have a prohibition system for cartels and, therefore, a system of notification and authorisation. We revised German cartel law at the beginning of 1999 to bring it more in line with European cartel law. This applies particularly to Art. 81(3), and we have just inserted a provision similar to Art. 81(3). I think that notification and authorisation procedures still have their advantages. The approach the Commission now proposes in the White Paper might lead to a certain change of culture in the assessment of horizontal restraints. When only clear-cut hard core cartels are clearly forbidden and everything else is more or less allowed, then companies might get the impression they can basically do anything they wish. We all know that it is quite difficult to obtain information about restrictive practices that go on in the market. This is especially true for restrictive horizontal agreements because the companies within the agreement have similar interests and therefore no reason to complain. Those who suffer from the restrictive agreements—cartel outsiders, customers and suppliers—often do not have sufficient knowledge of the anti-competitive behaviour to file a substantiated complaint. Therefore, the probability of receiving complaints because of restrictive horizontal agreements is not very high. The situation is different for vertical agreements because here the contracting parties (for example supplier and customer) do not necessarily have the same interests. I think, therefore, that it is still right and necessary for horizontal agreements to be notified, thus giving us the chance to have a look at them and if necessary have them modified so that they are less restrictive and will be suitable for an exemption.

As far as decentralisation as such is concerned I am fully in line with the Commission. I agree that it is absolutely necessary to decentralise the application of Art. 81(3) of the EC Treaty. As pointed out above the Bundeskartellamt already has some experience in the application of Arts. 81(1) and 82 of the EC Treaty. In particular, when applying 81(1) it is nearly always necessary for the possibility and

---

* Head of German and European Cartel Law Section, Bundeskartellamt, Germany. The views expressed are personal and do not necessarily represent the views of the Bundeskartellamt.

*J. Rivas and M. Horspool (eds), Modernisation and Decentralisation of EC Competition Law*, 89–91.
© 2000 *Kluwer Law International*.

probability of an exemption according to Art. 81(3) to be assessed. In cases the Bundeskartellamt has dealt with so far, an 'obstruction notification' has often been sent to the Commission. I use this term to describe a notification which has as its purpose to obstruct the Bundeskartellamt procedure without there being real prospect of obtaining an exemption. The companies concerned say to themselves: 'We will apply for an exemption even if we do not really see any possibility of being successful, but we just want to stop or delay the Bundeskartellamt procedure which would result in a prohibition'. In order to avoid such practices, I think it really would be necessary for national authorities to have the power to decide on exemptions according to Art. 81(3) of the EC Treaty.

I would like to turn to some of the problems caused by decentralisation which have already been addressed by others. Firstly I turn to the problem of how to achieve coherence when applying the law. I found the proposals by John Temple-Lang very interesting. In Germany we basically have the same problem. Besides the Bundeskartellamt there are 16 Länder Cartel Authorities which have the power to apply German cartel law. Seventeen different authorities therefore have to apply the same law and there are sometimes differences in interpretation. Nevertheless, so far we have not really experienced any major problems. We have a system of meetings twice a year to solve potential problems. The Bundeskartellamt and all the Länder Cartel Authorities meet for two days and discuss cases and legal problems. As far as I know, whenever there have been differences it has always been possible to solve them during these meetings. After a thorough discussion of the relevant legal problem or case the authorities decide which line to take. By this system we ensure coherence in the application of German cartel law.

As far as national courts are concerned, Germany has a system of specialised cartel law chambers within courts. In each of the 16 Bundesländer there is at least one specialised cartel law chamber which deals exclusively with problems of cartel law. All cases involving cartel law have to be brought before these chambers. This system seems to work rather well. The decisions of the cartel law chambers have to be sent to the Bundeskartellamt. Many of them are also published so that everyone knows which court has taken which decision. If there are discrepancies between the decisions of the different court chambers, the case may be brought before the specialised cartel chamber at the Federal Supreme Court, the Bundesgerichtshof. This is the highest court in Germany for matters of cartel law (comparable to the European Court of Justice for European cartel law). Differences between decisions of Länder cartel chambers are normally solved at this level. One could imagine a similar system throughout Europe where the European Court of Justice would be the final instance if a major problem of coherence arises.

Other problems do not seem to be that difficult to resolve, for example, that of the allocation of cases. The cases the Bundeskartellamt has dealt with so far under European cartel law were quite clearly national cases. They were cases where there was a small international component—otherwise they would not fall under Art. 81(1) of the EC Treaty—but they were so clearly focused in Germany that I do not think anybody ever questioned that the Bundeskartellamt would be the right authority to deal with these cases. We even had some complaints referred to us by the Commission, where it was also very clear that this was a case of mainly national importance so the national authority would be best placed to deal with it.

I do not know of any example where there has been a real problem concerning the allocation of a specific case.

Then there is the question of legal security if the White Paper system were to come into force. This, as far as I know from discussions with the German Federation of Industry, seems to be a real problem. Companies claim that they already only notify 'borderline' agreements when they are really not sure whether they fulfil the conditions of Art. 81(3). In clear cut cases, they tend not to notify, even at the present time, because a notification considerably delays the implementation of the agreement. I think, therefore, it would be desirable to have some sort of guidance for companies that are not sure whether their agreements fulfil the exemption criteria.

Another interesting problem is the question whether the procedure would be shorter if national authorities were competent to apply Art. 81(3) of the EC Treaty. Nicholas Green has said that the national authorities already have a full workload which would make it impossible for them to deal with additional cases within tight time frames. In my view, this concerns the decision-making procedures. In the Bundeskartellamt, for example, the procedure for coming to a decision is much easier than that of the Commission. Our decisions are taken by three people within the same department. Only prohibition decisions, some exemption decisions and 'phase 2' merger decisions have to be thoroughly reasoned *vis-à-vis* the notifying companies. In other cases (especially opposition procedures and 'phase I' merger decisions) an internal note signed by the decision-makers is sufficient. Thus the case handlers do not have to write a long and elaborate decision in every case of minor importance. In such cases they simply tell the companies to proceed without further ado. In my view, therefore, the decision-making procedure of the Bundeskartellamt could still be at least a little speedier than that of the Commission.

# Chapter Nine: The United Kingdom Competition Act: Issues of Due Process and Decentralisation

CHARLES BALMAIN*

## I. Introduction

The existing UK Competition regime will finally be replaced by an entirely new order of competition rules based extensively on the EC Competition system, on 1 March 2000. This paper investigates certain implications of the adoption by the UK of the Community's method of combating business delinquency. It identifies the features of the new Competition Act[1] which are most relevant to the ensuing discussion, and goes on to focus on the areas of legal professional privilege and the right to silence. Analysis is made of how these procedural safeguards are ensured at the EC level and, correspondingly, how they will be protected at the national level, after the entry into force of the Act. The paper will finally go on to examine certain implications of the adoption of the Commission's White Paper on the modernisation of the EC competition rules with reference to the Competition Act.

## II. The demise of the ancien regime

The body of UK legislation that the Competition Act is replacing, has long been criticised for its complexity and inefficiency at tackling anti-competitive behaviour.[2] This is a result, primarily, of the form-based approach to the classification of anti-competitive agreements taken by the Restrictive Trade Practices Act 1976. The competition regime being introduced is, in part, a reaction to the shortcomings of the existing system. It will be incorporated into domestic legislation by the Competition Act 1998,[3] which replaces the Restrictive Trade Practices Act 1976 and the Resale Prices Act 1976, and amends the Competition Act 1980.[4] Prior to the March 2000 starting date there has been a 16-month transitional period during which businesses have had the opportunity to adapt to the requirements of the new Act.[5]

The Competition Act introduces the so-called 'Chapter I' and 'Chapter II' Prohibitions onto the domestic statute-book. The Chapter I Prohibition is a prohibition of

---

\* White & Case, Brussels.
1 Henceforth, to be referred to as either the 'Competition Act,' 'CA' or the 'Act.'
2 For an example of such criticisms see: R. Whish: *Competition Law*, Butterworths, London, 1993, at the Appendix.
3 The Competition Act received Royal Assent on 9 November 1998.
4 Office of Fair Trading Guidelines to the Competition Act 1998, *OFT 400: The Major Provisions*, March 1999, London, p. 2.
5 Transitional Arrangements are provided for in Schedule 13 of the Competition Act.

*J. Rivas and M. Horspool (eds), Modernisation and Decentralisation of EC Competition Law*, 93–111.
© 2000 *Kluwer Law International*.

anti-competitive agreements, based strictly upon Art. 81 EC, whilst the Chapter II Prohibition is a replication of Art. 82 EC, prohibiting the abuse of a dominant position. Importantly, both prohibitions contain jurisdictional barriers, restricting their scope either to agreements implemented, or intended to be implemented within the UK,[6] or part thereof,[7] (Chapter I) or alternatively to the conduct of undertakings constituting an abuse of a dominant position which may effect trade within the UK[8] (Chapter II). In light of the Commission's White Paper calling for the decentralised application of Community competition rules, this jurisdictional delineation is likely to become of great importance.

Two points are of particular interest in relation to the analysis of the differing levels of procedural safeguard protection that will exist under the Community and UK systems. Firstly, the Act gives the Director General of Fair Trading investigative powers analogous to those currently enjoyed by the European Commission. The second aspect is the existence of Section 60. This is one of the most significant provisions of the Act, requiring that competition questions arising within the UK must be dealt with in a manner that is in conformity with the way in which such questions would be dealt at the Community level.

In light of the foregoing, it would seem that UK procedural safeguards applied in competition cases should be determined with reference to Community jurisprudence. It is by no means clear, however, that the UK Parliament intended to adopt a set of procedural rules which may be contradictory to fundamental principles of UK procedural law. Whether procedural safeguards under the Competition Act will go beyond those existing at the European level is a real issue which merits attention.

## III. The EC antitrust system: a suitable role model?

One of the defining characteristics of European Antitrust Procedure is the Commission's role as investigator, prosecutor and judge,[9] being responsible for the investigation and adoption of decisions censuring behaviour that infringes Arts. 81(1) or 82 EC. These multiple functions of the Commission may pose considerable risks to the rights of the defence.

In *Musique Diffusion Française*,[10] the applicants argued that this combination of roles within the Commission constituted a breach of essential procedural requirements. The Court of Justice held that, although the Commission was not a tribunal within the meaning of Art. 6(1) of the European Convention on Human Rights, it was nevertheless bound to respect those procedural safeguards guaranteed by Community law.[11] Thus, the Court confirmed that it was a fundamental principle of Community law that the right to a fair hearing should be observed in all proceedings, including those of an administrative nature.

---

6 Section 2(3) CA.

7 Section 2(7) CA.

8 Section 18(1) CA.

9 C.-D. Ehlermann and B. Drijber, *Legal Protection of Enterprises: Administrative Procedure, in Particular Access to the File and Confidentiality*, On file with the Author, at para 2.2.

10 Judgment of 7.6.83 in case 100-103/8 *SA Musique Diffusion Française* (*Pioneer*) v. *Commission* (ECR) 1825.

11 *Ibid.*, at paras 7 and 8.

J.M. Joshua, writing in 1994, also defended the Commission's position, observing that,

> There is no question of 'administrative justice' being a second class form of justice. Indeed, for a modern English administrative lawyer there is no contradiction in saying that an administrative authority determining a case has to do so 'judicially.'[12]

He went on to state that,

> One can and should expect such a body to act fairly and reasonably but it would be inappropriate to expect it to have the total detachment of a neutral judge.[13]

The House of Lords Select Committee on the European Communities observed in its 1993 Report into EC antitrust enforcement that structural change to divide the investigation, prosecution and decision-making functions within the Commission itself, was not necessary so long as adequate judicial control was in place.[14] It highlighted that such control could be provided by the Court of First Instance. This view is confirmed by that taken by Claus Dieter Ehlermann, who has observed that the fact that Commission Decisions are reviewable by the Court of First Instance (with full jurisdiction regarding the levels of fines) obviates any legal necessity for change in the structure of an administrative procedure.[15]

The fact that the UK has chosen to adopt an administrative system based on the Community approach, giving both investigatory and decision-making powers to the DGFT, will raise similar concerns for the rights of the defence as those experienced at the Community level. Whether the judicial review process being introduced is sufficient to dispel such concerns will be explored below.

## IV. The procedures adopted by the Competition Act

Under the terms of the Competition Act it is incumbent upon undertakings to notify agreements to the Director General of Fair Trading in order to obtain individual exemptions.[16] Undertakings may also be given the benefit of 'parallel exemption' by virtue of Section 10 of the Act. This will allow exemption in instances where an undertaking's agreement has already been covered by an individual exemption adopted by the Commission,[17] or would have been covered by a block exemption, had there been the necessary effect on inter-state trade.[18]

---

12 J.M. Joshua, *The Powers of The Commission*, in, *Droits de la Défense et Droits de la Commission dans le Droit Communautaire de la Concurrence*, Bruylant, Brussels, 1994, at p. 19.

13 *Ibid.*, also at p. 19.

14 The House of Lords Select Committee on the European Communities, *Enforcement of the Community Competition Rules*, Session 1993–94, 1st Report, Her Majesty's Stationery Office, London, at para 103.

15 C.-D. Ehlermann and B. Drijber, *op. cit.*, at para 2.2.

16 OFT 400, *The Major Provisions*, *op. cit.*, at p. 10.

17 This rule is subject to the qualification that the DGFT may impose conditions or cancel the benefit of parallel exemption if the agreement could produce, 'significant adverse effects on a market in the United Kingdom, or part of it,'—Office of Fair Trading Formal Consultation Draft: OFT 411, *The Draft Procedural Rules Proposed by the Director General of Fair Trading*, March 1999, London, Rule 21(1).

## 1. The investigatory procedure

It is the investigatory procedure to be adopted in instances of non-notification, however, that raises more important issues regarding due process. The Act gives powers of investigation to the DGFT which are analogous to those enjoyed by the Commission. Thus, an investigation may be triggered where the DGFT has 'reasonable grounds for suspecting' an infringement of the Chapter I or II Prohibitions, notably pursuant to a complaint.[19]

The powers of the DGFT in the course of an investigation are contained in Sections 26–29 of the Act. These are similar to those contained in Regulation 17/62, so that the DGFT may require, by written notice, a person to produce specified documents or information which he considers to be relevant to the investigation.[20] In addition, the DGFT may carry out on-site investigations, with or without a warrant.[21] In the instance that the investigating officer is carrying out an on-site investigation without a warrant, the undertaking will usually have been given two days' written notice of the event.[22] Alternatively, on-site investigations under warrant may take place in one of three circumstances. Firstly, where material has been requested but not produced.[23] Secondly, in the instance where it is feared that relevant material may be destroyed or altered.[24] Finally, a search under warrant may occur where, in a previous investigation attempt, the officer has failed to gain access to the premises.[25]

Notably, during an on-site investigation an investigating officer will, upon request, allow,

> a reasonable time for the occupier's legal adviser to arrive at the premises before the investigation continues, if the officer considers it reasonable to do so and if he is satisfied that such conditions as he considers it appropriate to impose in granting the occupier's request are, or will be, complied with.[26]

It is undesirable, perhaps, that such a fundamental safeguard for the protection of defendants' rights as access to legal advice should be left to the ultimate discretion of the officer in charge of the investigation into the very same defendants.

## 2. Infringement decisions

Following an investigation, the DGFT may adopt a statement of objections declaring the Chapter I or II Prohibitions to have been infringed.[27] In line with the

---

18  As will be seen below the DGFT will actively encourage undertakings whose agreements may infringe both the EC and UK rules to notify their agreements to the Commission since such exemption at the EC level will bring with it parallel exemption at the UK level. Moreover, the DGFT will give priority to agreements which have received a Comfort Letter from the Commission.

19  Section 25 CA.

20  Section 26(1) CA.

21  Sections 27 and 28 CA.

22  Section 27(2) (a) CA.

23  Section 28(1) (a) CA.

24  Section 28(1) (b) CA.

25  Section 28(1) (c) CA.

26  Office of Fair Trading Formal Consultation Draft: OFT 411, *The Draft Procedural Rules Proposed by the Director General of Fair Trading*, March 1999, London, Rule 13(1).

27  Section 31(1) CA.

Commission's practice of granting undertakings an Oral Hearing, there is an obligation on the DGFT to allow parties potentially effected by a decision to make representations to the DGFT.[28] If an infringement decision is subsequently adopted, Directions may be imposed as necessary, to bring that infringement to an end.[29] Where the imposition of Directions is deemed insufficient or inappropriate, Section 36 grants the DGFT the power to require the payment of a penalty.

As with the Community regime, that being introduced into the UK may be seen as a mixture of both administrative and criminal procedures in the sense that there is potentially a highly punitive effect resulting from infringement of the Prohibitions. Undertaking are exposed to potential fines of up to a maximum of 10% of annual turnover.[30] As with the Community, the DGFT may increase the level of a fine as a deterrent to the undertakings concerned and to others.[31]

## V. Judicial review under the Competition Act

In the UK, the new Competition Commission[32] will be responsible for hearing appeals. These may be made by any party whose agreement or conduct has been the subject of a decision by the DGFT.[33] Third parties may also appeal decisions of the DGFT before the Competition Commission, provided they can demonstrate to the Director General that they have sufficient interest in the decision.[34]

Appeals will be dealt with by Appeals Tribunals consisting of members of the Competition Commission appointed by the Secretary of State specifically for the fulfilment of the Commission's functions in relation to appeals.[35] Tribunals will have a wide range of powers in relation to appealed decisions, including the ability to confirm or set aside a decision of the DGFT.[36] Section 49 of the Act allows that decisions of an Appeal Tribunal may in turn be appealed to the 'appropriate court.'[37] This will be the Court of Appeal, hearing appeals on both points of law and on the levels of fines imposed by a decision of a tribunal.

Two points of comparison with the Court of First Instance merit attention. Firstly, as with the Court of First Instance, the Appeals Tribunals will not undertake any investigatory work and, if presented with significant new evidence by a party to an appeal, will refer the matter back to the DGFT.[38] Secondly, unlike the Court of First Instance, applications for appeal to an Appeals Tribunal must be made within

---

28 Section 31(2) (b) CA.
29 Sections 32(1) and 33(1) CA.
30 Section 36(8) CA.
31 Office of Fair Trading Guidelines to the Competition Act 1998, OFT 407, *Enforcement*, March 1999, London, point 4.2.
32 Created by virtue of Section 45(1) CA.
33 Section 46(1) CA. The Competition Commission will also take on the responsibilities of the former Monopolies and Mergers Commission.
34 Section 47(1) CA. The 'appropriate court' in Northern Ireland is the Court of Appeal and the Court of Session in Scotland.
35 Competition Act, Schedule 7, Part I, s. 2(1).
36 Competition Act, Schedule 8, Part I, s. 3(2).
37 Section 49(2) (a) CA.
38 OFT 400, *The Major Provisions, op. cit.*, point 14.5.

one month of the publication of a decision.[39] This is in comparison to the two months provided for by Art. 230(5) EC. Although this is a shorter period of time, it is difficult to see that this difference could seriously infringe the rights of the defence. Globally, the system of judicial review being introduced appears to be appropriate in providing an adequate level of review of the DGFT's actions.

## VI. Section 60: consistency with EC jurisprudence

Section 60 represents a highly innovative piece of legislation, adopting as it does, an entire body of EC principles and jurisprudence for use in the interpretation of the new UK competition regime. Lord Simon attempted to explain its rationale during the parliamentary debates on the Act, saying,

> The purpose of the governing principles clause is to ensure so far as possible that the UK and EC prohibitions are interpreted and develop consistently with the EC competition law system. This is of critical importance in minimising burdens on business.[40]

The provisions of Section 60 apply to all relevant UK authorities: the DGFT, the Competition Commission and domestic courts.[41]

Section 60(1) of the Act lays down the following general principle whereby,

> The purpose of this section is to ensure that *so far as is possible* (having regard to any relevant differences between the provisions concerned), questions arising under this Part in relation to competition within the United Kingdom are dealt with in a manner which is *consistent* with the treatment of corresponding questions arising in relation to competition within the Community.[42]

This is indicative of the UK's intention to harmonise the UK and EU antitrust regimes,[43] and represents a dramatic innovation in terms of the traditional Common Law approach to statutory interpretation, requiring guidance as to the interpretation of a domestic statute to be taken from Community jurisprudence.

Section 60(2) shows the extent of the duty to observe consistency, by requiring the DGFT (or any person acting on his behalf, and any court (or tribunal) when determining a question arising under Part I of the Act, to do so with a view to ensuring no inconsistency with:

> (b) the principles laid down by the Treaty and the European Court, *and any relevant decision of that Court*, as applicable at that time in determining any corresponding question arising in Community law.[44]

---

39 *Ibid.*, point 14.7.
40 Lord Simon, *Hansard*, 25.11.97, 1997, Column 960; quoted in: S. Goodman, *The Competition Act, Section 60—The Governing Principles Clause*, ECLR 1999, Issue 2, Sweet and Maxwell, London, at p. 73.
41 OFT, *The Major Provisions*, *op. cit.*, point 6.4.
42 Emphasis added.
43 M. Furse, *UK Competition Law, The Competition Act 1998*, Business Law Review, January 1999, at p. 11.
44 Section 60(2) (b) CA. Emphasis added.

Lastly, Section 60(3) requires regard to be had to the relevant decisions of the Commission. In this respect, it should be noted that Section 60 covers not only the Chapters I and II Prohibitions, but also the powers of investigation and enforcement in Part I Chapter III.

Crucially, there is scope for derogation from the principle of consistency. This can be found in the cautious wording of Section 60, requiring conformity only in 'so far as is possible.' Equally, Section 60(2) requires that courts (including tribunals and the DGFT) must act 'so far as is compatible with the provisions of this Part' to ensure no inconsistency. Thus, different approaches may occur. The paper will now examine two procedural safeguards, namely legal professional privilege and the right against self-incrimination, as possible instances in which inconsistencies can be expected.

## VII.  Legal professional privilege under EC law

The development and recognition of legal professional privilege is one of the significant bodies of jurisprudence developed by the ECJ in the field of competition. In all Member States, the principle that correspondence between lawyer and client ought to be privileged is guaranteed to some extent.[45]

In spite of this, Regulation 17/62 does not deal with the matter of the confidentiality of communications between lawyer and client. In response to complaints concerning the lack of due process in EC Antitrust law, however, the Commission and Court were forced to address the issue, adopting measures to afford a greater degree of protection to defendants.[46] This matter was specifically addressed in the *AM&S* case.[47] In this case the Court observed that,

As far as the protection of written communications between lawyer and client is concerned, it is apparent from the legal systems of the Member States that, although the principle of such protection is generally recognised, its scope and the criteria for applying it vary ...[48]

The Court went on to hold that Regulation 17/62 should be interpreted as giving protection comparable to that found in the Member States, subject to two specific restrictions. These were that,

... such communications are made for the purposes of and in the interests of the client's rights of defence and, ..., they emanate from independent lawyers, that is to say, lawyers who are not bound to the client by a relationship of employment.[49]

---

45 C. Harding, *European Community Investigations and Sanctions*, Leicester University Press, London and New York, 1993, at p. 29.

46 I. Van Bael, *A Practitioner's Guide to Due Process in EEC Antitrust and Antidumping Proceedings*, The International Lawyer, no. 4, vol. 18, at p. 841.

47 Judgment of 18.5.82 in case 155/79, *AM&S* v. *Commission*, (1982) ECR 1575.

48 *AM&S*, *op. cit.*, at para 19.

49 *Ibid.*, at para 21.

As a further condition, defendants subject to an investigation by the Commission under Art. 14 of Regulation 17/62, if claiming that information merited protection under the head of legal professional privilege, would have to provide, in the alternative, 'relevant material' demonstrating that the documents for which confidentiality was being claimed merited legal protection.[50] If disputes as to the nature of the documents for which privilege had been claimed arose, the Court gave the solution that the Commission could adopt an Art. 14(3) decision requiring the production of the relevant documents. That decision would be reviewable by the Court as an act of the Community under the terms of Art. 230(4) EC.

The *AM&S* decision provides a limited degree of privilege. However, it excludes from its ambit, the protection of in-house lawyers' communications, and those of lawyers based outside the European Union. In its 13th Report on Competition Policy, the Commission expressed its intention to redress this discrimination through the conclusion of bilateral international agreements with third countries so as to extend legal privilege to the lawyers of those countries.[51] However, the necessary agreements have not been concluded, and the matter would seem to lie dormant.[52]

The Court of First Instance confirmed and refined the *AM&S* decision in *Hilti*.[53] In this case, the applicant contended that internal documents reporting the contents of legal advice obtained by the undertaking from external lawyers, in the interests of their rights of defence, should benefit from the confidentiality which would be granted to the original information. To allow the Commission access to these internal memoranda, it was argued, would render the protection given to communications between undertakings and external legal advisors meaningless. Importantly, the Court accepted this reasoning, holding that,

> ... the principle of the protection of written communications between lawyer and client may not be frustrated on the sole ground that the content of those communications and of that legal advice was reported in documents internal to the undertaking.[54]

The European Courts' approach to the matter of privilege is in conflict with the UK's system of privilege, insofar as domestic lawyers may remain subject to the professional rules of the Bar Council or the Law Society whilst employed as in-house lawyers. This situation was alluded to in the *AM&S* judgment, when the Court recognised that, among the Member States' legal systems, there were primarily two reasons for affording professional privilege, either in recognition of the nature of the legal profession or for the more specific purpose of upholding the rights of the defence.[55] However, the Courts, by taking a restrictive approach, intended to guarantee the rights of the defence whilst adopting a level of protection they considered to be suitable in the context of competition proceedings.

---

50 *Ibid.*, at para 29.
51 Commission's 13th Report on Competition Policy, para 78.
52 L. Blanco, *EC Competition Procedure*, Clarendon Press, Oxford, 1996, at p. 135.
53 Judgment of 4.4.90 in case T-30/89, *Hilti* v. *Commission*, (1991) ECR-II 1439.
54 *Ibid.*, at para 18.
55 *AM&S, op. cit.*, at para 20.

## VIII.  Privilege in the United Kingdom

Unlike the EC competition rules, the Competition Act is not silent on the issue of legal professional privilege. Section 30(1) of the Act imposes a limitation on the powers of investigation enjoyed by the Director General of Fair Trading in that, either on written notice or during the course of an investigation, a person may refuse to disclose such information as constitutes a privileged communication.[56] Section 30(2) specifies what will be considered as privileged communications, providing that,

> 'Privileged Communication' means a communication—
>
> (a)  between a professional legal adviser and his client, or
> (b)  made in connection with, or in contemplation of, legal proceedings and for the purposes of those proceedings,
>
> which in proceedings in the High Court would be protected from disclosure on grounds of legal professional privilege.[57]

Thus, the Act makes reference to the rules of disclosure governing actions before the High Court. Consequently, the same level of protection will apply to investigations, as well as to private actions before the Courts.

The new Civil Procedure Rules introduced in the UK will have altered the discovery process. In material terms, however there will be no alteration to the existing law on legal professional privilege, since the new rules take the same approach as contained in the Rules of the Supreme Court (RSC) (also known as the White Book). These contain a wide-ranging duty to disclose documents. For this purpose, Order 24, Rule 2(1) provides that,

> ... the parties to an action between whom the pleadings are closed must make discovery by exchanging lists of documents ... which are or have been in [their] possession, custody or power relating to any matter in question between them in the action.[58]

Under the discovery process, parties to an action are under an obligation to list all documents, regardless of whether or not they were relied on by the party, including those for which privilege is claimed. Having identified the documents, each party has the right to inspect and take copies of all documents listed.[59] That right can be defeated if one of a number of conditions are met. Most relevantly, inspection will not occur if the party who made the disclosure has a concurrent right or duty to withhold such inspection.[60] Such a right is contained in the RSC in Order 24,

---

56  Office of Fair Trading Guidelines to the Competition Act 1998, OFT 404, *Powers of Investigation*, March 1999, London, points 6.1 and 6.2.
57  Section 30(2) CA.
58  Rules of the Supreme Court, Order 24, Rule 2 (O. 24, r. 2).
59  E. Fazzalari and P. Fortin, *Civil Justice in the Countries of the European Union*, Trenton Publishing, London, 1998, at p. 88.
60  Civil Procedure Rules, Part 31.3.

Rule 5(9) which brings all professional Solicitor–Client correspondence under the protection of legal professional privilege.[61] Crucially, Order 24, Rule 5(12) extends legal professional privilege to communications made between in-house lawyers, provided that the document at issue relates to legal rather than administrative matters.[62]

This confirms that the UK system gives a higher level of protection than the EC in the case of communications between external lawyers not based in a Member State and their clients, and in the case of communications between in-house lawyers and their employers on legal matters. This divergence has been recognised by the Office of Fair Trading in its guidelines to the Act, where it is stated that Community jurisprudence will not apply when the DGFT is carrying out investigations pursuant under the Chapters I or II Prohibitions.[63]

## IX. Self-incrimination

Unlike privilege afforded to lawyer–client communications, the Competition Act makes no reference to self-incrimination. It is unsurprising, therefore, that the Office of Fair Trading has indicated that,

> The defence against self-incrimination which has been recognised under EC jurisprudence will apply. Section 60 of the Act sets out principles which provide for the United Kingdom authorities to handle cases in such a way as to ensure consistency with Community law.[64]

Although seemingly straightforward, it is noteworthy that the adoption of the EC level of protection against self-incrimination may represent a significant departure from the national level of protection which will persist in non-competition instances, creating the situation whereby two concurrent bodies of law on self-incrimination will exist at the national level. This undesirable situation does have the advantage that businesses will be confronted with a consistent approach under both the EC and national competition rules.

## X. The EC rules on self-incrimination

As with legal professional privilege, Regulation 17/62 is silent on the issue of self-incrimination, leaving the development of this procedural safeguard up to the ECJ. It is accepted that the Council consciously omitted to include a right to silence in Regulation 17/62, fearing that its inclusion would undermine the investigatory powers being granted to the Commission.[65] The right against self-incrimination is recognised by all legal systems in the Member States to varying degrees. For this to be of relevance in EC competition proceedings such a right had to be shown to constitute a general principle of community law, extending to both legal and natural

---

61 RSC O. 24 r. 5(9).
62 RSC O. 24 r. 5(12).
63 OFT, *Powers of Investigation, op. cit.*, point 6.2.
64 OFT, *Powers of Investigation, op. cit.*, point 6.3.
65 For example, see Harding, *op. cit.*, at p. 27, or Joshua, *op. cit.*, at p. 34.

persons. Furthermore, that general principle had to be shown to extend beyond criminal proceedings to competition investigations and proceedings as well as preliminary administrative inquiries.[66]

The two cases of *Orkem*[67] and *Solvay*[68] arose following the adoption by the Commission of decisions requiring the production of information pursuant to Art. 11(5) of Regulation 17/62. The Commission required, *inter alia*, the parties to produce information pertaining to the manner in which they had fixed prices and quotas at meetings alleged to have taken place in the operation of a PVC cartel.[69]

In the cases, Advocate General Darmon noted that the determination of 'necessary information' in the sense of Art. 11 of Regulation 17/62 was a matter left to the discretion of the Commission.[70] He pointed out, however, that the investigative measures should not be excessive or disproportionate to the result to be achieved. On examining whether the right not to incriminate oneself constitutes a general principle of community law, AG Darmon stated that,

> Coercive machinery of … [the kind contained in Regulation 17/62] … appears to me intellectually incompatible with the right to silence.[71]

AG Darmon noted that, whilst there did appear to be a common principle in all Member States protecting the right to silence in criminal proceedings, it became 'progressively less common as one moves away from … classic criminal procedure.'[72] The Court was unable to conclude that, in the face of such diverse protection against self-incrimination amongst the Member States, such a right could be interpreted as existing in relation to Regulation 17/62.

It is worth noting Paul Lasok's observations in his critique of the *Orkem* and *Solvay* cases. Lasok identifies that Commission investigations are divided into preliminary and subsequent stages of enquiry. He concludes that, as both stages are carried out by the Commission, the defendant's procedural rights in the second stage could be prejudiced if no restrictions on the Commission's rights of investigation with respect to the first stage are in place.[73]

The Court in *Orkem* reiterated its earlier judgment in *National Panasonic*,[74] stating that the purpose of the preliminary investigation procedure was to enable the Commission to gain the information necessary to verify the 'existence and scope of a specific factual and legal situation.'[75] On the basis of that information, the Commission could determine whether to issue a statement of objections, commencing the procedure laid down in Regulation 99/63.[76]

---

66 Harding, *op. cit.*, also at p. 27.
67 Judgment of 18.10.89 in case 374/87, *Orkem* v. *Commission*, (1989) ECR 3283.
68 Judgment of 18.10.89 in case 27/88, *Solvay* v. *Commission*, (1989) ECR 3355.
69 P. Lasok, *The Privilege Against Self-Incrimination in Competition Cases*, 2 ECLR 1990, at p. 90.
70 Opinion of AG Darmon in case 374/87, *Orkem* v. *Commission*, *op. cit.*, at para 66.
71 *Ibid.*, at para 88.
72 *Ibid.*, at para 99.
73 Lasok, *op. cit.*, at p. 91.
74 Judgment of 26.6.80 in case 136/79, *National Panasonic (UK) Ltd.* v. *Commission*, (1980) ECR 2033.
75 *Orkem*, *op. cit.*, at para 21.
76 Commission Regulation 99/63 of 25 July 1963 has now been replaced by: Commission Regulation 2842/98 of 22 December 1998.

The Court also confirmed that Regulation 17 gives a minimum of procedural guarantees to undertakings in the course of the preliminary investigatory procedure.[77] This led the Court to examine the question of the possible application of a general Community right against self-incrimination in the context of the competition rules.[78] The Court could only find a general principle amongst Member States to grant a right to silence to natural persons in criminal proceedings.

Moreover, it held that Art. 6 of the European Convention on Human Rights does not contain a right to silence,[79] but that the need to safeguard the rights of the defence constituted a fundamental principle of the Community legal order. By approaching the issue from this angle the Court could show that,

> ... although certain rights of the defence relate only to contentious proceedings which follow the delivery of the statement of objections, other rights must be respected even during the preliminary inquiry,[80]

so as not to prejudice, at that stage, those rights of the defence which must be respected during administrative procedures which could give rise to the imposition of penalties.

Therefore, the Court upheld the Commission's right to request information contained in Art. 11 of Regulation 17/62, even to the extent of requesting information which could implicate the undertaking in question. It also established, however, that the Commission may not 'undermine the rights of defence of the undertaking concerned.'[81] This fundamental principle of the Community legal order, although not a right to silence, may obviate an undertaking's duty to provide information that could implicate them in anti-competitive conduct.[82]

*Orkem* and *Solvay* constitute a prohibition against the Commission's asking potentially inculpatory questions which would amount to an admission of the existence of a specific factual situation. A factual situation which it is, instead, up to the Commission itself to prove. This position has been reconfirmed in several cases, notably by the Court of First Instance in the *Société Générale*.[83]

The issue of the right to remain silent also arose in a referral from a Dutch court in the case of *Otto BV* v. *Postbank*.[84] The ECJ was asked to provide a preliminary ruling on whether a national court investigating an infringement of Arts. 81 or 82 must respect the rights of the defence as they were laid down in *Orkem* and *Solvay*.[85] The ECJ denied that Dutch Courts were obliged to respect the right to silence as embodied in Community jurisprudence, holding that national courts

---

77 For example, the Commission may only take a decision requiring the supply of certain information once a previous request has proved ineffective.
78 *Orkem, op. cit.*, at para 27 *et seq.*
79 *Ibid.*, at para 30.
80 *Orkem, op. cit.*, at para 33.
81 *Ibid.*, at para 34.
82 *Ibid.*, also at para 34.
83 Judgment of 8.3.95 in case T-34/93, *Société Générale* v. *Commission*, (1995) ECR II-0545.
84 Judgment of 10.11.93 in case C-60/92, *Otto BV* v. *Postbank*, (1993) ECR II-911.
85 T. Jestaedt, *The Right to Remain Silent*, in, *Droits de la Défense et Droits de la Commission dans le Droit Communautaire de la Concurrence*, Bruylant, Brussels, 1994, at p. 116.

should observe national procedural rules. It did observe, however, that the proceedings before the Dutch Court were civil proceedings, of a different nature to the administrative proceedings before the Commission.[86]

## XI. The right to silence under existing law in the United Kingdom

Under the Rules of the Supreme Court, Order 24 Rule 5(34), 'documents tending to criminate or expose to proceedings for a penalty... under the law of any part of the UK (Civil Evidence Act 1968, s. 14) need not be disclosed by a party.'[87] In such instances the risk of exposure to a penalty must be apparent to the Court, and real (*Renworth* v. *Stephanson* (1996) 3 AllER 244 CA).

In more detail, Section 14(1) of the Civil Evidence Act 1968 provides that,

> The right of *a person* in any legal proceedings *other than criminal proceedings* to refuse to answer any question or to produce any document or thing if to do so would tend to expose that person to proceedings for an offence or for the recovery of a penalty—(a) shall apply only as regards criminal offences under the law of any part of the United Kingdom *and penalties provided for by such law*; ...[88]

The case of *Rio Tinto Zinc*[89] (*RTZ*) is instructive in establishing the extent of application of this right to silence. In *RTZ*, the Court of Appeal established that the terms of Section 14(1) of the Civil Evidence Act applied where the information to be disclosed could lead to the exposure of the undertakings concerned to the possibility of proceedings under Art. 85(1) EC (now 81(1) EC). Lord Denning MR assessed the status of the EC competition rules in relation to the UK system of privilege against self-incrimination:

> It is plain, therefore, that Rio Tinto Zinc may be exposed to a very large fine by the European Commission. Is it a penalty? I think it is. It is a penalty for entering into an agreement to restrict competition or to fix prices contrary to Article 85. It is to be noted that Article 15, paragraph 4 of the General Regulations says: "The decisions taken under paragraphs 1 and 2 shall not entail any consequences under criminal law." ... So the fines are not enforceable by the sanctions of criminal law. Only by the civil procedures of the state. In this case, by the civil procedure of the English Courts. Nevertheless, they are clearly penalties just as much as the penalties under revenue law are penalties enforceable by civil procedures ... So liability to them is a ground for privilege against self-incrimination.[90]

Thus, evidence which might lead to the initiation of proceedings by the Commission is covered by the privilege against self-incrimination under the current UK laws. The House of Lords' decision in *RTZ* was followed by Graham, J. in *British Leyland*.[91]

---

86 *Ibid.*, at p. 117.
87 Rules of the Supreme Court, Order 24, rule 5(34).
88 Emphasis added.
89 *Rio Tinto Zinc Corporation and Others* v. *Westinghouse Electric Corporation*, (1978) AC 547.
90 As per Lord Denning MR, in *RTZ*, 1978 AC 565.
91 *British Leyland Motor Corp. Ltd.* v. *Wyatt Interpart Co. Ltd.*, (1979) 3 CMLR 79.

## XII. The implications of the Competition Act for the UK law on self-incrimination

During the Committee stage of the Competition Bill, Lord Simon stated that the incorporation of EC jurisprudence,

> extends not only to the substantive law but also to the general procedural safeguards developed under EC law; for example, the right against self-incrimination.[92]

This contrasts with point 4 of the DGFT's Draft Procedural Rules which states that,

> Section 60 does not require the UK authorities to follow the procedural practices of the EC Commission. The Director General of Fair Trading's procedural rules therefore do not need to be consistent with the practices of the EC Commission.[93]

It is contended that, whilst the DGFT is not bound to follow the precise schematic of procedural rules used by the Commission, it is obliged to follow the general principles of Community law,[94] unless the Act provides a specific derogation, as has been seen to be the case with legal professional privilege. This is borne out by the DGFT's guidelines which confirm concisely that, 'The defence against self-incrimination which has been recognised under EC jurisprudence will apply.'[95] Thus, the traditional domestic respect for the right to silence, is to be replaced by the jurisprudence of the ECJ.

## XIII. Inconsistency between the Competition Act, the Human Rights Act and EC jurisprudence

In November 1998, the UK adopted the Human Rights Act. This 'transforms' the substantive provisions of the European Convention on Human Rights into the domestic legal system.[96] Clause 3 of the Human Rights Act requires public authorities (including the Courts) to interpret legislation to be construed in a manner which is incompatible with the terms of the Convention in 'so far as it is possible to do so.' Thus, rights derived from the Convention are subordinate to existing or future statute-based obligations which are not compatible with those rights.[97]

---

92 Lord Simon, *Hansard*, 25.2.97, Column 960, quoted in S. Goodman, *The Competition Act, Section 60—the Governing Principles Clause*, ECLR 1999, Issue 2, Sweet and Maxwell, London, at p. 74.

93 OFT 411, *The Draft Procedural Rules Proposed by the Director General of Fair Trading, op. cit.*, point 4.

94 S. Goodman, *op. cit.*, at p. 74.

95 OFT 404, *Powers of Investigation, op. cit.*, point 6.3.

96 S. Greer, *A Guide to the Human Rights Act 1998*, European Law Review, February 1999, Sweet and Maxwell, London, at p. 3.

97 Stephen Grosz, Jack Beatson QC and Peter Duffy QC, *Human Rights, The 1998 Act and the European Convention*, January 2000, Sweet and Maxwell, London, at p. 9.

On a Community level there has long been a tension between the Human Rights Court in Strasbourg and the ECJ. In its Opinion 2/94 the ECJ denied that the Community is bound by the European Convention on Human Rights.[98] In the field of competition law this is reflected by the ECJ's failure to date to follow the position adopted by the European Court of Human Rights' in its *Funke*[99] judgment. In this case, the European Court of Human Rights explicitly confirmed that Art. 6(1) of the European Convention on Human Rights guarantees a right to silence in administrative proceedings.[100] To adopt this reasoning would doubtless erode the powers of investigation enjoyed by the Commission, at a time when the Commission itself is calling for the extension of its investigatory powers.[101] It is helpful to recall that the perceived need for extensive investigatory powers was the very reason for the omission of a right to silence in Regulation 17/62 in the first place.

Section 60 of the Competition Act, combined with the terms of clause 3 of the Human Rights Act, require the right to silence, as recognised by the ECJ to be applied in the UK. One may question the wisdom of incorporating a body of jurisprudence into the UK which is at odds with the European Convention on Human Rights.

It is to be hoped that the situation that this results in may increase pressure on the ECJ to bring its jurisprudence into line with that of the Strasbourg Court. This is all the more pressing when one takes into account that, under the terms of the Competition Act, a person may be guilty of a criminal offence punishable by a term of imprisonment not exceeding two years if he, 'intentionally obstructs an officer in the exercise of his powers under a warrant issued under Section 28.'[102] Whilst such sanctions are not available under Community law, they are also to be used against individuals should they intentionally obstruct an officer of the DGFT in the performance of an investigation under warrant ordered (or requested) by the Commission. Exposure to criminal liability makes coherent protection of the rights of the defence all the more pressing a priority.

Realignment of the Court's jurisprudence on the issue of the right to silence may be imminent. That the *Orkem* and *Solvay* jurisprudence was incompatible with the ECtHR's reasoning in *Funke* has been argued in a number of cases, notably by Ian Forrester QC before the Court of First Instance in the *Siderca* Case[103] (lodged before the CFI in January 1998). The Court's judgment in this case is still pending. This would be an ideal opportunity for the Court of First Instance to bring the jurisprudence on the right to silence into line with the European Court of Human Rights.

---

98 Opinion 2/94 of 28.3.96, on the Adhesion of the Community to the European Convention on Human Rights.

99 Judgment of the European Court of Human Rights of 25.2.93, in case 82/1991/334/407, *Funke/France*, Series A no. 256 A.

100 W. van Overbeek, *The Right to Remain Silent in Competition Investigations*, ECLR 1994, Issue 3, Sweet and Maxwell, London, at p. 129.

101 Commission White Paper on Modernisation of the Rules Implementing Arts. 85 and 86 of the EC Treaty, 1999/C 132/01, at paras 112 and 113.

102 Section 42(7) CA.

103 Case T 8/98, Siderca Sica v. *Commission*. My thanks go to Ian Forrester QC for this observation.

## XIV. The Commission White Paper and the Competition Act

The Commission's recent proposals to end the system of notification and autho-risation, decentralise the application of Community rules and intensify *ex post* control[104] of undertakings' behaviour raise several points of interest in relation to the Competition Act.

One of the stated goals of the Commission is to bring about the effective decentralised application of Community competition rules through,[105]

> a network of authorities operating on common principles and in close collaboration.

In this respect the Competition Act must be seen as an important step in that direction through the provision of an appropriate legislative framework, coupled, it is to be hoped, with the allocation of sufficient resources to ensure the effective application of both UK and Community Competition rules.

### 1. Jurisdictional delineation

The Competition Act takes a strictly implementation-based approach for the deter-mination of its jurisdictional scope.[106] This reflects the ECJ's jurisprudence in the *Woodpulp*[107] case by not going as far as to accept the existence of an effects-based doctrine. In the event that the effects-based doctrine becomes entrenched in EC jurisprudence, as would appear to be the case following the *Gencor judgment*,[108] the UK authorities will not follow suit. In this sense, the UK system defers to the EC system, recognising that an effect on inter-state trade places a matter within the competence of the Community. Ultimately, however, it is the mechanism by which the Community achieves decentralisation that will determine which cases are to be dealt with by the UK authorities.

Until such change is introduced, however, the Office of Fair Trading has recog-nised the likelihood of agreements overlapping between both systems. The DGFT is of the opinion that, under the current notification system, agreements which may fall within both the Chapter I Prohibition and Art. 81(1) should be notified to the Commission, so as to minimise compliance costs for undertakings.[109] Such a course of action is of benefit to undertakings as long as the Commission retains its monopoly over the grant of exemptions under Art. 81(3).

The abolition of the notification system and reliance on Community block exemptions to determine competition policy would obviate the requirement to notify agreements to the Commission. One of the risks in such a regime is that

---

104 Commission White Paper, *op. cit.*, at para 74.
105 *Ibid.*, at point 91.
106 Furse, *op. cit.*, at p. 13.
107 Judgment of the Court of 27.9.88 in joined cases 89, 104, 114, 116, 117 and 125 to 129/85, *A Ahlstrohm Osakeyhtio and others* v. *Commission*, (1988) ECR 5193.
108 Case T-102-96 *Gencor Ltd. v. Commission* (1999), ECR II-753.
109 Office of Fair Trading Guidelines to the Competition Act 1998, OFT 401, *The Chapter I Prohibition*, March 1999, London, point 7.1.

Member States will apply competition policy inconsistently. This makes the parallel exemption system introduced by Section 10 of the Act of great importance. This provision ensures that the UK authorities must respect the terms of Community block exemptions, thereby reducing the risk of inconsistencies.

## 2. Investigative powers

The Competition Act places the DGFT in an excellent position to fulfil a role of cooperation with DGIV. The Act expressly grants officials of the DGFT with the power to assist DGIV in its investigations. Section 61(2) provides that,

> For the purposes of a Director's investigation, an officer of the Director to whom an authorisation has been given has the powers of an official authorised by the Commission in connection with a Commission investigation under the relevant provision of Community law.[110]

In order to facilitate such investigations by DGFT officials on behalf of the Commission, the Act specifies that judges of the High Court may issue a warrant if they are satisfied that 'a Commission investigation is being, or is likely to be, obstructed.'[111] The question arises, therefore, of what level of procedural safeguards ought to be observed by the DGFT in the course of such investigations.

It is interesting to note that, in the course of investigations undertaken by the DGFT on behalf of the Commission, legal professional privilege may only be claimed for communications which would fall within the scope of privilege recognised by the jurisprudence of the Court of Justice.[112] Officials of the DGFT must truly be seen as acting in a Community capacity, in the course of their assisting the Commission with its investigations.

Thus, it is vital that the exact nature of the investigation is clear. One can envisage the situation whereby information may be made available to officials of the DGFT in their capacity as Commission investigators which, whilst it may not be of use in relation to a case under Arts. 81 or 82, may be relevant under the Chapters I or II Prohibitions, but which would not be available to the investigators under the rules of privilege governing domestic investigations. Information obtained in the course of a Community investigation, should therefore, not be used for the purposes of a domestic case. This issue will not arise in relation to self-incriminatory documentation, as the UK system, as was seen earlier, is to be governed from the outset according to the ECJ's jurisprudence on the matter.

With respect to the foregoing, it is of particular note that the Commission has proposed to increase its powers of enquiry, notably by ensuring the right of the Commission to question undertakings' representatives or staff during investigations,[113] and to summon representatives to the Commission's premises to provide

---

110  Section 61(2) CA.
111  Section 62(1) CA.
112  OFT 404, *Powers of Investigation, op. cit.*, point 10.8.
113  Commission White Paper, *op. cit.*, at point 113.

information.[114] Such extensive powers undoubtedly pose increased risks to the rights of the defence. They do not correspond to the powers which have been granted to the DGFT, and would further increase the disparity between Community and national investigations.

As Mario Siragusa has observed,[115] the fact that legal professional privilege does not cover in-house counsel could mean that in-house lawyers would be summoned by the Commission to provide information on internal legal advice. Given the increased onus on businesses that would result from *ex post* control, and the corresponding reliance on in-house counsel, it is imperative that any modifications to the Commission's procedure must bring in-house counsel within the scope of legal professional privilege recognised by the Community.

## XV. The role of National Courts

The White Paper calls on National Courts to play an enhanced role in the application of the Community competition rules, allowing applicants to invoke the direct applicability of Art. 81(3) in court proceedings.[116]

In the UK, courts may already apply Arts. 81 and 82 EC by virtue of their direct effect, as recognised by the ECJ in *BRT* v. *Sabam*.[117] This is reinforced by the Commission Notice of 1993 on Cooperation between National Courts and the Commission.[118] Point 18 provided that, in the case of civil proceedings for damages for violation of either Art. 85(1) (now Art. 81(1)) or 86 (now Art. 82), or in actions relating to the validity of contracts under Art. 85(2) (now Art. 81(2)),

> ... the direct effect of Article 85(1) and Article 86 gives national courts sufficient powers to comply with their obligations to hand down judgment.[119]

Despite this, the UK courts have shown themselves reluctant to accept arguments based upon EC competition rules. Julian Maitland-Walker, examining three UK cases decided in 1998, all of which incorporated EC competition arguments, observed that the Court of Appeal (in two instances), and the High Court in the other, avoided giving judgments based on the strength of seemingly legitimate arguments concerning the violation of Art. 81(1).[120]

The Office of Fair Trading, in its guidelines on the application of the Act explicitly recognises that third parties who have suffered loss as a result of unlawful

---

114 *Ibid.*, at point 114.
115 Mario Siragusa, *A Critical Review of the White Paper on the Reform of the EC Competition Law Enforcement Rules*, Paper given at the 26th Annual Fordham Conference on International Antitrust Law and Policy.
116 Commission White Paper, *op. cit.*, at point 100.
117 Judgment of the Court in case 127/73, *Belgische Radio en Televisie (BRT)* v. *SV Sabam*, (1974) ECR 51.
118 Commission Notice of 13.2.93, on Cooperation Between National Courts and the Commission in applying Arts. 85 and 86 of the EEC Treaty, (1983) OJ no. C 39/6.
119 *Ibid.*, at point 18.
120 J. Maitland-Walker, *Have English Courts gone too far in Challenging the Effectiveness of EC Competition Law?* ECLR 1999, Issue 1, Sweet and Maxwell, London, at p. 4.

agreements or conduct may have a legitimate claim for damages in the Courts.[120] Such a right is not provided for in the Act, since the Government felt that such a reference to a third party right to damages was unnecessary.[121] The increased ability of the Courts to accept competition-based arguments will be vital if applicants are to be permitted to raise arguments based on the applicability of Art. 81(3).

## XVI. Conclusion

It is hoped that the foregoing discussion will have shown that the transition from the UK's existing system of competition rules to that being introduced by the Competition Act is a positive step. The paper has focused on the difficulties likely to be experienced in the area of due process. The essence of the Competition Act is, however, the attempt it has made to replicate the EC system at a national level. It is precisely in the area of procedural law, therefore, that most problems can be expected to arise, since the Act attempts to accommodate an entirely new enforcement regime within existing domestic rules of procedure.

The situation will be created in which the DGFT and his officers will be forced to observe the EC system of legal professional privilege when conducting investigations on behalf of the Commission and the UK rules in domestic situations. This raises an important point with respect to the decentralised application of the Community competition rules, namely, that in a decentralised system the allocation of cases which are purely national or which are Community cases dealt with by national competition authorities must be consistent between the Member States. In addition there must be a clear distinction by national authorities between the correct procedural rules to follow when acting on behalf of the Community, and those to be followed when acting in a domestic context.

It has been seen that the Competition Act permits differences in procedural rules to be followed by the DGFT in a Community or domestic context. To permit such differences between national competition authorities acting on behalf of the Community in a decentralised system would, however, pose a great risk to the uniform application of EC competition rules.

---

120  OFT 407, *Enforcement, op. cit.*, point 5.1.
121  Furse, *op. cit.*, at p. 13.

# Chapter Ten: The Effects of the White Paper on the Dutch Competition Act

JOOST HAANS*

## I. Introduction

The Dutch Competition Act[1] (the 'DCA') was adopted on 22 May 1997 and entered into force on 1 January 1998. This Act reflects the change of economic thinking in The Netherlands.

The former Acts on competition of 1935, 1941 and 1956 were all based on the reasoning that too much competition may be harmful to economic welfare and that it was desirable to stimulate co-operation. These Acts therefore incorporated a so-called abuse-system. Under this system anti-competitive behaviour as such was allowed, unless it was explicitly prohibited, after a lengthy procedure, by the Ministry of Economic Affairs. For this reason, The Netherlands was often referred to as cartel paradise.

Now this has all changed. In line with the developments throughout Europe, The Netherlands have adopted a Competition Act, modelled on EC Competition Law.

I shall give a brief overview of the provisions of the DCA that deal with the prohibition of cartels, the prohibition of the abuse of a dominant position and the system of merger control.

In The Netherlands the execution of the Competition Act is entrusted to the Dutch Competition Authority[2] (the 'NMa'). I shall briefly look into the tasks and powers of the NMa in the various procedures.

Finally, I shall discuss some aspects of the White Paper on Modernisation of the Rules implementing Arts. 81 and 82 of the EC Treaty and the official reaction of the Dutch government regarding this White Paper. In conclusion, I shall discuss some influences the White Paper may have on the DCA.

## II. Cartel prohibition

Art. 6(1) DCA reflects the same underlying general principle as Art. 81(1) EC Treaty. Art. 6(1) reads as follows:

> Agreements between undertakings, decisions by associations of undertakings and concerted practices by undertakings which have as their object or effect the

---

* Van Bael & Bellis, Brussels.
1 De Mededingingswet.
2 Nederlandse Mededingingsautoriteit.

*J. Rivas and M. Horspool (eds), Modernisation and Decentralisation of EC Competition Law*, 113–122.
© 2000 *Kluwer Law International.*

prevention, restriction or distortion of competition within the Dutch market, or any part thereof, are prohibited.

It is clear that this provision is based on Art. 81(1) EC Treaty from the fact that Art. 1 DCA explicitly states that the words 'agreement', 'undertaking', 'association of undertakings' and 'concerted practices' should be understood in the sense of Art. 81(1) EC Treaty.

According to Art. 6(2) DCA, agreements and decisions prohibited pursuant to para 1 are legally null and void.

Although it is obvious that Art. 6(1) DCA is intended to have a meaning very similar to Art. 81(1) EC Treaty, there remains an important difference between these two articles which excludes the possibility of copying the Art. 81(1) EC Treaty case law into the application of the DCA. Contrary to the EC Treaty, the DCA, clearly does not contain as a condition for its application that trade between Member States must be affected. Art. 6(1) DCA merely requires that the practices have effect 'within the Dutch market or any part thereof'. In addition, since the EC Treaty and the DCA do not share the same objectives, it is not in all cases possible to apply the same teleological interpretation to Art. 81(1) EC Treaty and Art. 6(1) DCA. An important objective of the EC competition rules is the realisation of the Common Market. This is, however, not a direct objective of the DCA, whose main objective is the realisation of the benefits of free competition to the Dutch economy. Therefore, one cannot blindly apply all the case law that relates to Art. 81(1) EC Treaty to Art. 6(1) DCA.[3] As was stated by the Dutch legislator: 'The DCA is based on the EC Treaty, but is not a copy of it'.

## 1. Appreciable effect

Similar to the application of the competition rules under the EC Treaty, the DCA envisages to prohibit anti-competitive agreements which have an appreciable effect on competition. The criteria which may determine this under EC law can be used as guidance for the application of Art. 6(1) DCA.

Contrary to the EC Treaty, the DCA itself has a *de minimis* rule. Art. 7 DCA contains thresholds which are considerably lower than those set out in the *de minimis* Notice of the Commission. According to Art. 7 DCA, the prohibition of Art. 6(1) DCA shall not apply to agreements, decisions and concerted practices if there are not more than eight undertakings involved and if the aggregated turnover of the undertakings concerned does not exceed 10 million guilders (approximately 4.5 million Euro) if the undertakings concerned are mainly involved in the supply of goods, or if the aggregated turnover does not exceed two million guilders (approximately 0.9 million Euro) in all other cases. According to Art. 7(3) DCA, the *de minimis* rule may be declared applicable to agreements which, from a competition point of view, are clearly of minor importance. Such exclusion from the scope of

---

3 See W. VerLoren van Themaat, 'The Dutch Competition Act of May 22, 1997', (1997) European Competition Law Review, vol. 18, issue 6.

Art. 6(1) DCA by general administrative order is preferable to the *ad hoc* system of interpretation by the Commission, since the former system is likely to enhance legal clarity and security.

Art. 6(1) DCA also does not apply to restraints which are ancillary to a concentration (Art. 10 DCA). According to Art. 11 DCA, which is comparable to Art. 86(2) EC Treaty and states that Art. 6(1) DCA shall not apply where one of the undertakings concerned is entrusted with the operation of services of general economic interest in so far as the application of Art. 6 prevents the performance of those special tasks. Art. 12 DCA declares Art. 6(1) DCA inapplicable to agreements, decisions and concerted practices to which Art. 81(1) EC Treaty does not apply pursuant to a Council Regulation or a Commission block exemption Regulation. According to Art. 13 DCA the EC block exemption Regulations apply also where there is no possible effect on inter-state trade, but if this was the case, the exemption by Regulation would apply. Art. 14 DCA states that agreements which benefit from an individual exemption pursuant to Art. 81(3) EC Treaty shall not be caught by Art. 6(1) DCA. In addition to the EC block exemption Regulations, Art. 15 DCA grants the Dutch legislator the possibility to adopt national block exemptions by administrative order. To date four national block exemptions have been adopted. These are:

—Exemption concerning combination agreements between two or more undertakings concerning tenders;
—Exemption concerning agreements to protect a sector of business in new shopping centres;
—Exemption concerning co-operation agreements in retail trade; and
—Exemption concerning temporary agreements on prices of the daily press.

## 2. Individual exemption

Art. 17 DCA offers the director general of the NMa the possibility to grant an individual exemption to the prohibition of Art. 6(1) DCA. Art. 17 DCA is identical to Art. 81(3) EC Treaty. It is noteworthy that pursuant to Art. 4(2) DCA, the Minister of Economic Affairs may issue general instructions to the director general as to how certain non-economic interests should be considered when deciding on granting an individual exemption.

The procedural rules concerning the exemption are laid down in Arts. 18–23 DCA. Contrary to the procedure with the Commission which knows no fixed time limits, Art. 19 DCA states that the director general is to decide on the request for an exemption within four months. This period can be extended with another four months. Also on the request of extension of the individual exemption, the director general has to decide within four months (Art. 22 DCA). However, the DCA provides no sanction where these time limits are exceeded. According to Art. 21(2) DCA certain restrictions can be attached to an exemption and also the grant of an exemption can be made subject to the provision that certain conditions are met. Art. 20 DCA states that the decision granting the exemption may be made effective retroactively, but not prior to the date on which the application for exemption was received. Art. 15(2) of Regulation 17 states that if such conditions attached to an exemption under the EC competition rules are not met, a fine can be imposed. It is remarkable that the DCA does not contain a similar provision.

## III. Abuse of a dominant position

The DCA deals with this issue in just two Arts. (24 and 25).

Art. 24 DCA states that undertakings are prohibited from abusing a dominant position. Art. 1 DCA defines what is to be understood by a dominant position. It states:

> A position of one or more undertakings which enables those undertakings to prevent effective competition being maintained in the Dutch market or any part thereof by giving them the power to behave to an appreciable extent independently of their competitors, suppliers, customers or their end users.

Although it is clear that this definition is based on ECJ and CFI jurisprudence and Commission decisions, contrary to the definitions concerning Art. 6 DCA, this definition makes no explicit reference to Art. 82 EC Treaty. Therefore, this definition does not imply that the EC definition and its development will be binding in the application of the DCA.

It is interesting that this definition includes the issue of collective dominance by referring to a dominant position held by more undertakings.

The DCA does not provide a definition of what constitutes an 'abuse'. Although the Explanatory Memorandum to the Act states that this term should be understood in the sense of Art. 82 EC Treaty, it would have been clearer if this was incorporated in the Act. On the other hand, it is also stated in the Explanatory Memorandum that the legislator wants to develop a national practice.

According to Art. 24(2) DCA, the realisation of a concentration shall not be deemed to be an abuse of a dominant position.

Art. 25 DCA states that the director general can declare Art. 24 DCA inapplicable where the application of Art. 24 DCA may interfere with the performance of services of general economic interest. This Art. is comparable to Art. 86(2) EC Treaty. An important difference, however, is that under Art. 25 DCA, the director general shall only make such a declaration on request and not automatically.

## IV. Concentrations

The DCA introduces to Dutch law a system of merger control, which is based on the EC Merger Regulation. Prior to the present DCA there was no system of preventive supervision of concentrations under Dutch law. As a consequence, concentrations which did not have a Community dimension could not be prohibited.

Chapter Five (Arts. 26–49) of the DCA deals with the control on concentrations.

Art. 27 DCA distinguishes three types of concentrations: (a) the merger of two or more previously mutually independent undertakings, (b) the acquisition of direct or indirect control, and (c) the establishment of a joint venture, which performs all the functions of an autonomous economic entity on a lasting basis. Although the DCA is modelled on the EC Merger Regulation, it does not directly refer to this Regulation. Therefore, if the Act is to follow changes to the EC Merger Regulation it can do so only by amending the DCA. Since the DCA has not been adapted to the amendments of Art. 3(2) of the Merger Regulation, which entered into force on 1 March 1998,[4] the DCA still distinguishes between concentrative and co-operative joint ventures. As a result, Chapter Five of the DCA does not apply to joint ventures which give rise to the co-ordination of the competitive behaviour of the founding undertakings.

An important consequence of this is that co-ordinative joint ventures do not benefit from the stricter time limits that apply in the case of concentration control. Failure to respect these time limits leads automatically to the decision that no licence is required or to the granting of such a licence. As mentioned before, the failure to respect time limits applicable to the procedure in relation to Art. 6 DCA does not have similar consequences.

According to Art. 28 DCA some situations shall not be deemed to constitute a concentration. It is clear that this Art. is based on Art. 3(5) of the Merger Regulation.

As a consequence of the 'one-stop-shop'-principle, Art. 33(1) DCA provides that the provisions of this Act shall not apply to concentrations which are subject to the supervision of the Commission.

## 1. Notification

If a proposed concentration falls within the scope of application of the DCA, it must be notified to the NMa. According to Art. 29 DCA, a concentration falls within the scope of the application of the supervision if the combined turnover of the participating undertakings in the preceding year exceeded 250 million Dutch guilders (approximately 112.6 million Euro) and at least 30 million Dutch guilders (approximately 13.5 million Euro) of which was realised in The Netherlands by at least two of the undertakings concerned.

Within four weeks of the receipt of this notification, the director general must decide whether he has reason to assume that the concentration will create or strengthen a dominant position which may restrict competition in the Dutch market. If so, the concentration requires a licence (Art. 37 DCA). Such a licence can only be obtained following a separate submission of an application. From that moment the investigation enters its second stage. This approach is different from the Merger Regulation where only one notification is required.

If the director general does not decide within four weeks, the concentration is deemed not to require a licence. Although, this short and straightforward rule seems favourable, it must be noted that according to Art. 38 DCA, the director general may suspend this period when he requires more information. This suspension shall last until the day on which such information is provided. The director general has full discretion in deciding exactly when this is the case.

A concentration may not be realised before a licence is obtained (Art. 34 DCA). It is noteworthy that, whereas the EC Merger Regulation requires a more or less

---

4  Council Regulation (EC) 1310/97 of 30 June 1997, of L/80/1997, pp. 1–6.

irrevocable agreement before the notification can be made, under the DCA, however, a notification can already be made from the moment of intention to merge.

The issuing of a licence can be made subject to restrictions or conditions (Art. 41 DCA). If a concentration is realised prior to this, it will be declared null. This nullity may be invoked by any concerned competitor or other party before a Dutch court.

The DCA provides for two exceptions to the requirement of prior notification. First, under Art. 39 DCA, prior notification is not required in the case of a public acquisition or exchange bid aimed at the acquisition of a share in the capital of an undertaking. Second, according to Art. 40 DCA, the director general may allow the realisation of a concentration before the licence is obtained for serious reasons, on request of the notifying party. Conditions may be attached to such a dispensation decision.

An important consequence of the procedure under the DCA is that, due to the simplified procedure in the first stage, concentrations which are obviously not anti-competitive will be cleared relatively quickly and easy. On the other hand, this simplified first stage procedure will have the effect that in some cases a licence will be required, which would not have been the case if an assessment was made on the basis of serious doubts, as required by Art. 6(1) of the Merger Regulation.

If the director general decides that a licence is required, the NMa has to decide in the second stage within 13 weeks after the application for a licence (Art. 44(1) DCA). Also in this stage, the director general may on the ground of serious reasons grant dispensation from the prohibition of realising the concentration before the licence is granted.

Art. 47 DCA regulates the political power of the Minister of Economic Affairs if the director general has refused to grant a licence. This provision, which does not have an equivalent in Community law, states that the Minister may, upon request, decide that the licence shall be granted if this is necessary for serious reasons in the general interest, which outweigh the expected restriction of competition. The term 'serious reasons in the general interest' refers to all kinds of policy considerations which are considered to be more important than effective competition in the Dutch market. It is noteworthy that the director general has stated that he can hardly imagine the Minister giving instructions in individual cases. The Minister of Economic Affairs at the time of the adoption of the DCA has confirmed not to have intentions to make use of the possibility provided by Art. 47 DCA. So far the Minister has kept his word.

As with the entire DCA, the system of supervision of concentrations is to comply as far as possible with the European system. However, with regards to the supervision of concentrations, the DCA provides no clear notion of the role of Community competition law. Also, it provides little guidance on how to deal with the divergence of the national system and the European model. It will be mainly to the Dutch courts, and maybe ultimately to the ECJ to decide on this.

## V. The Dutch competition authority

The enforcement of the DCA is entrusted to the NMa. The NMa operates under the Minister of Economic Affairs. The NMa is headed by the director general. Although formally the NMa is part of the Ministry, it is often referred to as an 'internal independent' authority or as an 'external part of the Ministry'. This independent character of the NMa is accentuated by the physical separation from the Ministry. The NMa is located elsewhere in The Hague.

The NMa has a staff of over 70 officials. These officials are appointed by the director general.

Before entering the decision-making procedure, the DCA distinguishes between the supervision and investigation procedure. Supervision is the control on the compliance with the DCA, without true research being undertaken with regard to a possible violation of the DCA. If there are reasons to believe that the DCA is violated, the investigation procedure can come into effect. Investigation is defined as: 'Actions taken in view of determining whether or not a violation has taken place'. Both procedures are carried out by the same officials. This implies that the same officials shall decide whether, as a result of supervision, there are grounds to start an investigation procedure.

Next, contrary to Commission practice, Art. 3 DCA introduces two stages in the decision-making procedure, thus separating certain powers within the NMa. According to Art. 3(2) DCA, officials who were involved in the investigation procedure and the drawing up of the report concerning the alleged infringement, may not be involved in the hearing of the parties and may also not be involved in the imposition of a fine. This Art. aims at ensuring the objectivity of the procedure by assigning different officials to different stages of the procedure. However, it must not be forgotten that the entire procedure remains with one authority, headed by one director general.

According to the Arts. 50, 52 and 56 DCA, the director general decides on the fine and is responsible for the supervision and investigation procedure. This is remarkable since several other Member States, such as Belgium, France, Germany and Great Britain have adopted a system where either the authority to sanction is given to another independent body, or to officials who fulfil certain special qualifications.

In any case, the Dutch legislator has eliminated the possibility of one case-handler being solely in charge of a file from beginning to end.

## VI. Reform of the enforcement of competition rules

On 28 April 1999, the Commission adopted the White Paper on Modernisation of the Rules Implementing Arts. 81 and 82 of the EC Treaty. According to the Commission this White Paper proposes a new, more efficient system of application of EU competition rules which will be suitable for the European Union of the future.

The Commission proposes the introduction of a directly applicable exception system. This has three elements: The ending of the system of notification and authorisation, decentralised application of competition rules, and intensified *ex post* control. In other words, the Commission proposes the abolition of the notification and exemption system laid down in the present Regulation 17 of 1962. It proposes to send the Council a proposal for a new Regulation which would render Art. 81 EC Treaty in its entirety directly applicable by the Commission, national competition authorities and national courts. As a consequence, the Commission would no longer hold the monopoly to grant exemptions under Art. 81(3) EC Treaty. Also, the Commission is of the opinion that the proposed changes will allow it to concentrate its resources on the most serious restrictions of competition, which are almost never notified.

One of the greatest concerns in relation to the proposed changes is that decentralisation may lead to incoherence. In a directly applicable exception system, the legislative framework is of primary importance. The application of the rules must be sufficiently reliable and consistent to allow business to assess whether their restrictive practices are lawful. Under the proposal, the Commission would keep the sole right to propose legislative texts and would act whenever necessary in order to ensure consistency and uniformity in the application of the competition rules.

In its official reaction to the White Paper, the Dutch Minister of Economic Affairs stated that uniformity is one of the most important concerns.

To ensure uniformity and consistency of competition policy, made at the Community level, the Commission has proposed that the amended Regulation 17 should include an obligation on the national competition authorities to inform the Commission of cases in which Arts. 81 and 82 EC Treaty are applied by the national competition authorities. Also, the national authorities would also be required to inform the Commission, on their own initiative or at the Commission's request, of any proceedings they were conducting under national law that might have implications for Community proceedings. The Commission would also have to be informed if an authority planned to withdraw the benefit of a block exemption. In addition, the Commission would still have the possibility of taking a case out of the jurisdiction of the national competition authorities.

With regard to the national courts, the Commission has proposed that these courts should be required to supply information to the Commission concerning proceedings in which Arts. 81 and 82 EC Treaty are invoked. This in order to maintain consistency of interpretation.

Following the Commission's intention to focus its resources on the most serious restrictions of competition, complaints will take on even greater importance than at present. Therefore, the lodging of complaints should be encouraged and facilitated. One important proposal is the introduction of a time limit of four months within which the Commission must inform the complainant of whether the Commission will take up the complaint or not. According to the proposal, if the Commission decides not to act, the complainant may challenge this decision before the Court of First Instance.

## 1. Comments

The above mentioned proposals, which are only a selection from the White Paper, may very well be essential for the achievement of the Commission objectives. However, the following comments might be taken into consideration.

The core objective of the Commission appears to be that it can spend more time and resources on dealing with serious violations of competition law. Therefore, the essential question is whether this will result from the proposals in the White Paper. To ensure uniformity and consistency, the Commission wants to be informed of the application of Arts. 81 and 82 by all the national authorities and national courts. Naturally, the review of all this information will also take up time and resources. Also, providing this information will put a constraint on time and resources of the national authorities and courts.

Under Dutch law, only in exceptional cases, will the Commission be allowed to intervene in a matter before a Dutch civil court. This can of course be amended by an EC Regulation. Such interventions will put another burden on the time and resources available to the Commission.

Also other aspects of the proposed decentralisation may save time and resources with the Commission, but will also shift the requirement to devote time and resources to the national authorities and courts. The argument by the Commission that national authorities have better knowledge of the national markets does not seem too valid. It seems highly unlikely that national authorities do not have to devote time and resources to get acquainted with the specific market and the players.

In The Netherlands the workload of the civil courts is already enormous, as in most—if not all—Member States, and it does not seem that these courts have additional capacity to deal with extra competition law cases as a result of the proposed decentralisation. The Commission has offered to assist national courts with certain problems. Again, this can take up considerable amounts of the Commission's time and resources.

The Commission has also stated that the national courts are closer to the European citizens. Indeed, the proximity of a national court and the language may very well be comfortable, but can hardly be considered a decisive argument.

In any case, the application of hundreds of national courts of—in particular—Art. 81(3) EC Treaty does not appear favourable to uniformity and consistency. Especially, since it does not seem likely that the Commission can get actively involved in every matter that raises a relevant question. Also, the preliminary procedure with the Court of Justice, which is the ultimate way for uniformity and consistency, provides often not a realistic alternative due to the length of the procedure.

The abolishment of the notification requirement appears to be favourable to undertakings, which no longer have to deal with this administrative burden. However, in a situation where either the Commission or a national authority might not be convinced of the application of Art. 81(3), the undertaking concerned might have less legal security than under the system of notification.

Another concern for undertakings under the new proposed system might be the issue of confidentiality. In a decentralised system, the transfer of files between authorities and between authorities and the Commission will be significant. This transfer should be somehow controlled in order to ensure confidentiality.

## VII. Conclusion

In the comment on the White Paper, the Dutch Minister of Economic Affairs stated that: 'Since the DCA is based on the European model, changes in this model shall therefore also be felt in the DCA'.

It is however important to note that the DCA is not a copy of the EC model and that in fact, the DCA is based on the EC rules in three different ways.[5]

First, in some areas, the DCA explicitly refers to the EC rules. This is the case in Art. 1, sub. e, f, g and h DCA in which certain terms are declared to be understood in the sense of the EC Treaty. Also, Arts. 12 and 13 explicitly state that Art. 6(1) DCA shall not apply when an EC block exemption Regulation is applicable. Regarding these provisions, the DCA has fully incorporated the aforementioned EC rules. Therefore, any changes in these EC rules will automatically be implemented in the DCA.

Second, certain rules of the DCA may be (almost) identical to the relevant EC rules, but, since they make no explicit reference to these EC rules, their meaning can deviate from that of the EC rules. Although it is the intention of the Dutch legislator to follow closely the EC rules, there is no such obligation stemming from the DCA. Therefore, changes in the meaning of EC rules resulting from the White Paper, may be held to have a different meaning than (almost) identically worded articles in the DCA.

Third, the DCA contains rules which are merely inspired by EC rules, but may be considerably different. An example is the procedure regarding Merger control. It is obvious that there is no obligation to follow EC rules in interpreting these DCA provisions.

As mentioned above, in the reaction to the White Paper, one of the main concerns of the Dutch government was uniformity, which might suffer from the different interpretation of EC rules by the various national authorities and courts. This concern might also apply to the unequal impact the changes of EC rules might have on the various DCA provisions. Regarding some issues a Dutch court must identically, and with regard of uniformity throughout the Community, interpret EC and DCA rules, whilst regarding other issues he may or may not decide to apply a different interpretation.

I agree that, as has been said, the DCA and the EC Treaty have different objectives and that the Dutch economy may have specific characteristics which may justify a different interpretation, but I seriously wonder if different interpretations would be beneficial to the legal certainty of undertakings operating on the Dutch market, and therefore beneficial to the Dutch economy. Therefore, while respecting the objectives of the EC Treaty and the DCA, the NMa and Dutch courts should in interpreting all DCA provisions consider the interpretation given to the EC rules.

---

5 See M.M. Slotboom, 'De Mededingingswet: niet met handen en voeten gebonden aan het EG-recht', SEW (1999) February.

# Chapter Eleven: The Experience of National Authorities: Spain

EDUARDO PRIETO KESSLER*

This article sets out to provide a brief overview of the competition system in Spain. This is of particular relevance at the moment because of the current interest in how competition law is to be applied by different types of authorities, under different procedures and in different markets. The article will concentrate on the Spanish experience in the application of EC law by both national authorities and courts. I will conclude by making a personal assessment of the Commission's White Paper on modernisation.

## I. The competition system in Spain: institutions and legislation

Although Spain did not join the European Community until 1986, Spanish competition legislation has been based on EC norms since 1963, when the first Competition Act was enacted.

In 1989 a new Competition Act was enacted, it was based on the EC model. The two institutions that control the Spanish system are the Competition Defence Tribunal ('the Tribunal') and the Competition Defence Service ('the Servicio').

Competition procedures for infringements of the law consist of one single procedure divided into two seperate steps, one before the Servicio and the second before the Tribunal.

### 1. The Servicio

The Servicio is part of the General Directorate for Economic Policy and Competition Protection under the Ministry of Economy and Finance, with two different departments, one for restrictive practices, and the other for merger control. It is responsible for enforcement and refers cases to the Tribunal. It is also responsible for the proceedings and investigation of cases, and when it finds evidence demonstrating that the Competition Act has been violated, it presents a Statement of Objections to the presumed violators. The procedure finishes when the Servicio sends the file to the Tribunal with a report and a preliminary legal assessment. The Servicio may close a file at any point in an investigation with a formal decision, subject to appeal to the Tribunal; it may also reject a complaint with a formal decision, which is also subject to appeal.

### 2. The Tribunal

The Tribunal is an independent administrative body entrusted with competition law *quasi-judicial* functions. It resolves any questions that are placed before it by

---

* Deputy Director, Ministerio de Económica y defensa de la Competencia, Spain.

*J. Rivas and M. Horspool (eds), Modernisation and Decentralisation of EC Competition Law*, 123–128.
© 2000 *Kluwer Law International.*

the Servicio. It can issue orders to cease and desist, it can fine a firm's directors and senior management and can also fine a company up to 10% of it's annual turnover. The Tribunal is also empowered to issue interim measures at the request of the Servicio. Tribunal decisions can be appealed to the Chamber of Administrative Litigation of the National Court.

The 1989 Competition Act establishes a prohibition system very similar to the EC model, which includes a prohibition against anti-competitive agreements (Art. 1 of the SCA) and abuse of dominant position (Art. 6), modelled on Arts. 81(1) and 82 of the Treaty, and an authorisation system modelled on Art. 81(3). Art. 7 of the Competition Act prohibits unfair practices when they distort competition and may affect the public interest.

Anti-competitive agreements are prohibited from the date of their conclusion (prohibition principle), and their compatibility depends on an administrative decision. Some of the more noteworthy differences with EC competition law are:

- There is no explicit mention of the concept of Undertaking as the subject of the agreement or concerted practices in Art. 1.1 of SCA.
- A broader definition of the types of conduct which may be caught by Art. 1.
- The so called legal exemption included in Art. 2 of the SCA., which provides that any anti-competitive conduct, which in theory should be caught by the prohibition of Art. 1.1, may be exempted if it is authorised by enabling legislation.

The authorisation system is based on the criteria established in Art. 81(3). Authorisation may also be granted if it is in the general economic or public interest. The Government may adopt individual authorisations and Block Exemptions using these criteria as a base. No Block Exemptions, other than those already adopted by the European Community have yet been granted, meaning that Community Block Exemption Regulations (BERs) have been translated word for word into the Spanish legislation. From the legal point of view we can assume that Spanish provisions for competition protection are very similar to EC provisions.

This is not the case when we come to the procedures for application of the legislation. In general we could say that proceedings are much stricter at national than community level. A few examples:

- At national level all parties are allowed full access to the file, except for separate files containing business secrets.
- Competition bodies are obliged to issue a formal decision.
- Time limits. Investigation procedures of the Servicio are subject to a deadline of 18 months and the Tribunal has 12 months to adopt a decision once it receives the report from the Servicio.
- Means of appeal. Every decision of both institutions is subject to revision. The Tribunal revises the Service's decisions such as appeals against termination of procedures or against the close of an investigation. The Chamber of Administrative Litigation of the National Court revises Tribunal's decisions at jurisdictional level.

### 3. Conclusion

The Spanish competition legislation and the scope of its application, is very similar to that of the European Union. Nonetheless there are important differences such as the division of the procedure between two different institutions, or the stricter procedure under the national system.

## II. Application of EC Competition law by National Authorities

A relevant question when analysing the application by National Competition Authorities ('NCAs') of European Competition legislation is whether they use express legislation to apply EC law. In this sense the Spanish Competition Authorities (the Tribunal and the Servicio) were first authorised to apply EC competition rules in 1986 under Royal Decree 1882/86.

In 1998 a new Royal Decree was enacted (295/98) based on the new Competition Act, setting a '*ratione materiae*' attribution of powers to the Competition Authorities. Under the new provision the Tribunal is the competent authority that deals with the application of Arts. 81(1) and 82 in Spain, whereas, the Servicio is the competent authority that carries out investigations pursuant to Arts. 81(1) and 82 and collaborates with the Commission in terms of Art. 13 of Regulation 17/62. It also specifies the procedure that will be followed in relation to national proceedings when applying Arts. 81 and 82.

Making use of these powers the Tribunal has taken decisions in 38 cases under Art. 81, 22 cases under Art. 82 and 44 cases in application of the Broad Exemption Regulations. In this sense we consider that there has been a vigorous application of EC Competition law by the Spanish Competition Authorities. The main features of these applications have been firstly, that EC competition law has been applied jointly with the relevant Spanish law, which, as we have already stated, is very close in content to EC law. Secondly, continuous references have been made to Community cases and to European Court of Justice case law.

The parallel application of both Arts. 1 and 6 of the Spanish Competition Act and of Arts. 81 and 82 of the Treaty, and the continuous referrals to EU jurisprudence has resulted in certain uniformity in the application of EEC competition legislation by our national authorities. They have reached conclusions very similar to those the Community Authorities would have reached. This does not prevent the existence of various difficulties and obstacles in the application of EC legislation by National Authorities that prevent companies and lawyers from using it in the national field. In brief, we find the following difficulties in the application of EC rules by the Spanish authorities.

- EC legislation does not imply either a broader or a narrower interpretation of the prohibition system than the national legislation and therefore the NCA does not need to apply EC law to tackle anti-competitive practices.
- If EC law is applied, the decisions of NCA are more likely to be reviewed by the Commission, taking into consideration the powers given by Art. 9(3) of Regulation 17/62. Therefore, the NCA may prefer to just apply national law.

- If EC law is applied, a quick response may be endangered by the need of co-ordination with the Commission. The main reason is that whereas national proceedings are subject to time limits (18 months for the Servicio and 12 for the Tribunal to issue a formal decision), decisions at the Community level are not which means they usually take more time. Therefore, the likelihood of dilatory notifications increases. This also acts as a deterrent for the application of the EC legislation.

One final and important problem that needs to be looked at in relation to the application of EC law by national authorities is the *risk of inconsistencies* in the interpretation of the EC legislation between Community and national authorities. This is one of the issues that insufficiently dealt with in the Commission White Paper and deserves a deeper analysis if the decentralisation process proposed by the Commission is going to succeed.

There are some, though not enough, mechanisms, which have the objective of preventing the inconsistent application of EC competition law:

At community level we have:

- Art. 9(3) of the Regulation 17/62, and
- The Notice on Co-operation between the NCAs and the Commission.

At national level Art. 44 of the Spanish Competition Act states that in order to avoid possible conflicts of competence, in the event of a concurrent process before EC institutions (i.e., the Commission), the Competition Tribunal may postpone its final decision with regard to national law, provided that documentary evidence corroborates the fact that EC institutions are reviewing a case file with similar facts. In such a case, the suspension will be lifted only when the EC institutions have made a final judgement on the same matter. In general co-operation usually works well, although it should be further strengthened in a vertical and horizontal manner, that is, with both the Commission and other Member States' authorities.

### III. Application of EC law by National Courts

The risk of inconsistencies is nonetheless much greater when we come to the application of EC law by the national courts. This is a particularly sensitive area as shown by the lack of unanimity among authors and has fostered a broad doctrinal dispute as to whether national courts can apply EC rules or not.

Despite the doctrine of direct effect with regard to Arts. 81(1) and 82 of the EC Treaty, Spanish national courts have rarely applied EC competition rules, and even preliminary rulings under Art. 234 have been placed before the ECJ by our Competition Tribunal, which, as we have already stated, is an administrative body. The main reason is to be found in a judgement of our Supreme Court ('SC') (1993) where the SC recognised the direct effect of Arts. 81(1) and 82, but denied their direct applicability in Spain through the ordinary civil courts, reserving the application of these articles to the Competition Tribunal and the EC Commission. The SC stated that the civil courts should apply these articles where they are incidental to the main legal points being considered but not where they themselves make up the crux of the case being dealt with.

The SC takes into consideration, a peculiarity of our system; under Art. 13 of the Spanish Competition Act, in order to exercise a private suit before a civil court and recover damages caused by an infringement of the SCA prohibitions, a preliminary decision by the administrative jurisdiction, that is, the Tribunal and the National Court on appeal, is needed. Although the interpretation of this provision by the Supreme Court has varied depending on the author involved, and disregarding the fact that that this judgement does not preclude the direct application by the civil courts of EC competition legislation, the fact is, there has been a notable negative attitude by both Spanish courts and lawyers towards the civil courts dealing with Arts. 81(1) and 82.

The result of this approach is that Spanish Judges and courts are not familiar with competition law. Considering the Commission's proposal on decentralisation and strengthening of the national courts' role in the application of EC competition legislation, it is easy to foresee many problems in the near future in relation to the effective application of EC competition law by the Spanish courts.

## IV. The Commission's White Paper on the modernisation of competition rules

The need for reform is clear, the present system suffers from various problems. The main ones being:

- The Commission's monopoly for the application of Art. 81(3), which sets a duality of procedure.
- The lack of an adequate procedure under Regulation 17.
- The inefficient functioning of the notification system. It imposed an unnecessary administrative burden on both companies and on the Commission, without yielding the expected results in terms of being a source of information on restrictive practices or in terms of guaranteeing legal certainty for companies, as most notifications end without a formal decision.

The Commission's proposals seem to be sensible although the White Paper lacks a deeper economic analysis of other options. On the positive side the proposed reform will ensure the following:

- Competition authorities, especially DG Competition will be able to take away the need for notifications, which, as I said before, have lost much of their previous value, freeing resources for the tracing of more serious infringements.
- The whole of Art. 81 will be directly applicable and this will put an end to dilatory practices.
- NCAs will apply EC competition law more frequently since their procedures will no longer be subject to termination by virtue of prior action by the Commission. This will hopefully lead to a greater convergence in the application of competition law throughout Europe.
- It will reinforce the role of the courts in the preservation of individual rights derived from the infringement of competition rules, and it will therefore enable

NCAs to focus on competition problems related to the safeguard of the public interest.

- The reform should give us an opportunity to revise and improve the Com-mission's procedures under Regulation 17, such as the introduction of time limits (the deadline of four months to answer a complaint is a positive step in this regard), removal of restraints to full co-operation within the future network of NCAs (free movement of evidence), and procedural reforms.

On the negative side I will highlight the following:

- The lack of legal certainty for companies and their capacity to make accurate assessments of their agreements in the light of Art. 81(3).
- The difficulty in establishing a sufficiently clear legal framework for the correct interpretation of the new block exemptions and guidelines.
- The problems relating to the diverse interpretation of Arts. 81 and 82 among different National Authorities and between them and the Commission.
- The different procedures among member states and the danger of forum shopping derived from them.
- The difficulty in clarifying the relationship between the courts and the administrative bodies in relation to the application of EC and national competition legislation.

Despite all of these problems, this reform is urgently needed, and though it is challenging this magnificent opportunity to improve the law and encourage a more efficient and competitive markets must be taken.

# Chapter Twelve: United Kingdom Reaction to the White Paper

GRAHAM WINTON[1]

I am most grateful to have the opportunity to take part in this discussion on behalf of the Office of Fair Trading, and I have been very interested to hear the views expressed already on the Commission's White Paper by representatives from DG Competition and from other leading European competition authorities. I would like to use the time available to offer some brief thoughts on the main elements of the Commission's proposals and their implications for national competition authorities. Before I go any further I should issue the customary disclaimer, namely that my comments do not necessarily represent the official views of the Director General of Fair Trading.

The consultation period on the White Paper is of course still open, and the Government's views are therefore still being developed in the light of both consultation with interested parties in the UK, and our discussions with the Commission and other Member States in Brussels. But I can say at the outset that our approach to those discussions is a positive one. The recent DTI White Paper on Consumer Affairs says that 'the Government believes these proposals could bring about significant improvements to the competition regime'. It is clear from the Commission's White Paper that the factors which are driving DG Competition towards a new approach, in particular its desire to concentrate its resources on the investigation of serious breaches of competition law, have much in common with the way in which the UK authorities intend to operate the new Competition Act—something we will be hearing more about this afternoon.

One point about the OFT's own plans which is already well-known to practitioners is our desire to keep notifications to a minimum. Other Member States' experience with notifications has varied a good deal, both in terms of the number received, and the part they play in enforcement. From the point of view of a competition authority, two main reasons are commonly given for having a notification system. Firstly, it is said that notifications are useful because they provide information about the kinds of agreement which companies are entering into in the marketplace, information which can be used as the basis for policy decisions. While this may be true to some extent, I think it is questionable whether it provides sufficient justification for maintaining a system which imposes such high costs on both businesses and competition authorities. Secondly, it is suggested that the requirement to notify

---

1 Head of International Section, Competition Policy Division, Office of Fair Trading. The views expressed are personal, and do not necessarily represent the views of the Director General of Fair Trading.

*J. Rivas and M. Horspool (eds), Modernisation and Decentralisation of EC Competition Law*, 129–131.
© 2000 *Kluwer Law International*.

encourages companies to take account in advance of the concerns of competition authorities and to respect the law when entering into agreements. Again there may be some truth in this, but one thing which is certain is that competition authorities do not learn much about serious anti-competitive behaviour from notifications, for the simple reason that companies tend not to notify price-fixing and market-sharing agreements. So we are inclined to agree with the Commission's favoured option of scrapping the notification system.

It follows that we share DG Competition's reservations about the other main option for reform—the abolition of the Commission's monopoly on the granting of Art. 81(3) exemptions. As the White Paper rightly points out, this option—originally proposed by the Bundeskartellamt—would not *reduce* the total number of notifications, but rather would *redistribute* the caseload between the Commission and Member State authorities. Although the way in which cases would be allocated between authorities under such a system has not been worked out in any detail, it is reasonable to foresee that the distribution between national authorities might be uneven, and that the UK might expect to find itself with more than its fair share. This would obviously run counter to the policy I have described, of doing our best to discourage notifications under our own legislation so that we can concentrate on what we see as more important issues.

I have focussed, perhaps rather selfishly, on the effect of this kind of decentralisation on the OFT. But the point is a more general one—redistributing cases, many of which are of little real concern to anyone, is not, in our view at least, the answer. The use of measures such as block exemptions has had some effect in limiting the number of notifications, but—as the Commission itself has acknowledged in its Green Paper on vertical restraints—it has brought about problems of its own. So, while we agree to a large extent with the Bundeskartellamt's analysis of the problem, and the need to find a solution to it, we tend to agree with the Commission that a more radical approach is called for.

I said that our initial approach to the Commission's proposals was a positive one. But it has to be acknowledged that there are some complex technical and policy issues to be addressed. It is not clear how the Commission's proposed new system, without notifications, could operate alongside national regimes, such as that in the UK, with a notification system. It is clear from the initial reactions to the Commission's proposals that some companies attach importance to legal certainty of the kind that they can get if DG Competition provides a comfort letter—or even an exemption—following a notification to Brussels. Deprived of that possibility, will these companies simply turn to national authorities instead? While the Commission's proposals would not oblige Member States to abolish their notification systems, in practice I would suggest that there would be a lot to be said for uniformity at European and national level.

For the proposed new system to work, all national competition authorities will have to be given the power to apply Arts. 81 and 82 directly. In the UK, as in a number of other Member States, that would require a change to domestic legislation. That can be a difficult and lengthy political process. A decentralised system would clearly give rise to complex issues of which authority should deal with any given case, and how to ensure consistency in enforcement and analysis. It should not be beyond the Commission to devise systems for allocating cases between authorities and promoting consistency, but we should not underestimate the practical problems, both for businesses and competition authorities, which will have to be overcome.

Whatever system is eventually adopted, the move towards greater uniformity of legislation across Europe, and all Member States' growing experience of enforcing competition law, seem certain to lead to decentralisation to a greater or lesser extent. This will place a high premium on co-operation between Member States and the Commission. There is of course already a Commission notice on this issue, published in 1997. But, from my perspective as a Member State official with responsibility for liaison with the Commission on cases under Arts. 81 and 82, I would suggest that the notice has yet to have any significant effect in terms of our establishing detailed procedures for consultation and exchange of information. This is the case despite the fact that we fully accept the principles described in the notice. I should stress that this is an observation rather than a criticism. The OFT— and I know this is also true of other national competition authorities—has excellent informal lines of communication with DG Competition, and we have so far generally managed to co-operate quite effectively when, for example, the question has arisen of whether a particular case is best pursued at a national or a European level, or we have needed to ensure that actions which each of us was proposing to take do not conflict with each other. The principle of close and constant liaisons referred to in both Regulation 17 and the co-operation notice is, therefore, already a reality. It works to our mutual advantage and also, I think, to the benefit of the businesses with whom we deal, by reducing duplication of effort and the risk of divergent outcomes. But it is clear to me that, as the European and domestic regimes become more closely aligned with each other, this informal approach will need to be replaced by a more systematic one if we and the Commission are to continue to work effectively together.

Finally—while discussion of the White Paper has so far centred on the abolition of the notification system and the decentralisation proposals—there is plenty of scope for debate in some of the more detailed procedural changes which are contemplated, such as those on powers of investigation, a possible expanded role for the Advisory Committee of Member States, and the exchange of confidential information. Since the opportunity to undertake a major reform of this kind seems to occur only once in a generation, DG Competition can be forgiven for wanting to make it as comprehensive as possible. It will not be easy, though, to convince everyone of the merits of everything which has been proposed.

Notwithstanding all these challenges, though, the OFT will continue to play a constructive part in the consultation process which is now underway, with a view to creating a new European regime within which both DG Competition and national authorities can work effectively to deter anti-competitive behaviour.

# Chapter Thirteen: Modernisation and Decentralisation

JOHN SWIFT*

Thank you, Mr. Chairman, ladies and gentlemen. I am also in an odd position here because I am not a representative of a member state appearing on the panel, and unlike the other two speakers who started off with an apology I am not apologising for the state of the railways.

This is called a White Paper and White Papers in the UK normally lead to legislation within a fairly short time after their formulation. Railways again being an exception! The time limit for response to the Commission's White Paper is pretty tight and I think a question you might want to put to John Temple-Lang is whether there has been a process of consultation with the member states which gives John and his colleagues confidence that this White Paper will move forward into the legislation which everybody recognises is necessary in order to carry it through. I want to say briefly, does this proposal meet Professor Tesauro's aim? Does the proposed system reconcile the objectives of effective decentralisation with rigorous and uniform application of community competition law throughout all the member states? And if, by the way I have formulated that question, you indicate you have inferred some degree of scepticism you have it right. This is not about decentralisation, this is about concurrency, this is about conferring on other bodies the power to take certain types of decision which are currently allowed only to one. So let us not talk about decentralisation and removing the burden of decision making from the Commission into the Member States, it is nothing of the kind. I will make two points:

First the Commission recognise that through this measure they will have a greater ability to investigate those agreements falling within Art. 81(1) which in their view are wholly incompatible with the common market and should be identified and scrapped. That is a major public law enforcement role.

The second, and this was spoken to this morning with great honesty by John Temple-Lang and that is if the national authorities have got a problem they can always come to us, and if the national authorities want to refer matters to us, then they can do that as well. So here you have within a system which is supposed to promote decentralisation and modernisation, a system that, unless it is properly taken through, is going to finish up with a muddle. Has any cost–benefit analysis been applied to this kind of change? Is there any burden on the tax payer? What benefit is there to consumers? What benefit is there to undertakings? Is it likely to promote the more efficient allocation of resources within the community and the identification and prohibition of bad cartels? I doubt it.

---

* Head of Chambers, Monckton Chambers, London. Rail Regulator, 1993–1998.

*J. Rivas and M. Horspool (eds), Modernisation and Decentralisation of EC Competition Law*, 133–134.
© 2000 *Kluwer Law International.*

Is it likely to have a serious and significant financial benefit to lawyers, to economists, I don't doubt that!

Let me tell you what I have no problem with. I have no problem with the concept of an agreement or practice which is to be tested against its compatibility with the common market. That seems to me a sensible concept and one that is capable of being implemented by the national courts. I do not see any difficulty in cases being presented where the court has to resolve the whole of the issue, whether an agreement which for example involves exclusive distribution and is compatible with the common market, by putting together the two limbs of Art. 81(1). What I do have problems with if I am an undertaking, and I am looking at the 15 jurisdictions, is am I certain that by entering into these new agreements I am going to be acting within the law?

The basic problem here is one of hybridity. Old Arts. 85 and 86 not only have direct affect within the member states and create rights in favour of individuals but they are also the means by which a community policy to prohibit cartels and prohibit abuse of the dominant position are maintained. Now this element of private law and public law activities of Arts. 81 and 82 are essential to the implementation of these rules of the Treaty, but when you shift one executive decision making responsibility from one group of the European Commission into a set of groups that have then got to be linked together in some way, this measure has got to be thought through very, very carefully before you run the serious risk of taking away legal certainly. This is the biggest issue and the biggest problem in the whole of this development. Does it really have an adverse affect on legal certainly?

I think there are doubts, I would strongly urge all member states to think very carefully on the programme of implementation and on the project plan that really does secure the objectives that Professor Tesauro seeks to attain.

# European Business Law and Practice Series

Kluwer Law International – The Hague / London / Boston